A Christian Mind

Thoughts on Life and Truth

in Jesus Christ

by

Tom Gilson

Dedication

This work is gratefully dedicated to the many great friends who have been active commenters on the *Thinking Christian* blog for all these years — including the loyal opposition. The list is long:

Alex Dawson, AdamHazzard, Andrew W, Andy, Ardoise, bigbird, Bill L, Bill R, BillT, Billy Squibs, Bob Seidensticker (even with the snark), Brap Gronk, brgulker, Bryan, chapman55k, Charlie, Crude, d, Daniel, Dave, David Ellis, David Heddle, David Marshall, David P, Dirkvg, DJC, doctor(logic), Doug, Doug Peters, Melissa, DR84, drj, Fleegman, Franklin Mason, G. Rodrigues, Gavin, Geoff Arnold, GM, Grace, GrahamH, Greg Magarshak, Irenicus, Holopupenko, Jacob, Jacob Stump, JAD, JB Chappell, Jeanette, Jenna Black, JJS P.Eng, John Moore, Jordan, justaguy, Justin, kaapstorm, Keith, Kevin Winters, lambda.calc, Larry Tanner, Luke, mattghg, MedicineMan, Melissa, Mike, MikeAnthony, MikeGene, Mr. X, Neil Shenvi, Nick Matzke, Nick Peters, Oisin, olegt, ordinary seeker, Paul, Otto, Patrick Reynolds, Phil Torres, Philmonomer, Ray Ingles, Raz, Richard Wein, Rob, Roger, ryan, Sault, scbrownlhrm, Scott, Shane Fletcher, Skep, Stephen, Steve Drake, SteveK, TFBW, The Deuce, Thomas Reid, toddes, Tom Clark, Tom Graffagnino, Tony Hoffman, Victoria, William Bradford, woodchuck64. And more.

I would have listed several of the more frequent and otherwise important ones among you first, but I really couldn't decide how to draw that line in just the right place. You know who you are, and I hope you know how much I appreciate you, along with everyone who's participated in keeping the site such a lively place.

Our conversations have often been vigorous, sometimes contentious, always interesting. I've often wished I could sit across a table at Starbucks with each of you, including even those of you who have disagreed mightily with me. I'm pretty sure we'd have a respectful and open conversation, as I did once many years ago over breakfast with my all-time top atheist opponent on this blog, doctor(logic).

One thing that's always surprised me along the way is how many commenters here have been Ph.D. physical scientists. I'm a music and psychology major myself, but somehow the blog community has seemed like a comfortable home for many in the hard sciences.

A personal word to doctor(logic), by the way: You told me enough about yourself that morning, by dinnertime I knew your workplace, your title, your full name and much of your history. I could have phoned you at work. But you didn't want me revealing your identity, so I haven't and I won't.

While I'm thinking about it, though, I can't resist sharing how much I enjoyed the moment when you walked up to me in the hotel lobby, and I asked, "Doctor Logic, I presume?"

I enjoyed our time together, and I'd love to do more of the same with others.

Acknowledgements

Heartfelt appreciation goes to Lisa Gosling for invaluable help in proofing and arranging this manuscript. It helps that she's my daughter. But she's good at it, too, and she stepped in to help marvelously on short notice. Any errors in the manuscript are my own, re-introduced after she finished her work on it.

Thank you also to my wonderful wife, Sara Gilson, for putting up with my reactions while answering comments on the blog. ("Tom, you're sighing again!")

Thank you to Tim McGrew not only for the Foreword but also for suggesting the title for the book, for catching some last typos, and for being such a great encourager.

Thank you to Campus Crusade for Christ (its name at the time, now Cru), Ratio Christi, and now *The Stream* for letting this thinking be part of my vocation during my years of working with you.

Thank you to canva.com for the cover design elements.

Contents

Foreword

by Timothy McGrew

Thinking is hard work. More specifically, thinking *well* about *deep issues* is hard work.

What passes for thinking in everyday life isn't hard, but it also isn't very deep. We skitter along on the surface of the great ocean of ideas, paying our bills, making plans for dinner, choosing the next movie to watch – not bad things in themselves, but all things we can do without reflecting on the big questions. *Why am I here? Where am I going? What really matters?*

Christianity offers answers to these questions, and one of the first steps toward understanding Christianity is to know what those answers are. But that is only a first step. To think well requires us to see the implications below the surface, to connect things that seemed at first unrelated. Discovering hidden relationships between deep truth and daily life changes the way we see *everything*.

But where should we start? How can we recognize those connections? Most of us flounder about like inexperienced swimmers, fumbling and gasping and trying to blink the spray out of our eyes. We need to learn what it means to be thinking Christians. And we learn best not by thrashing around blindly but by following someone who can show us how it is done.

Tom Gilson has been thinking hard and writing well about the implications of a Christian worldview for decades. He sees true connections that are not obvious, and he knows how to show us their importance. Any Christian can tell you that Jesus is good, and that Jesus is powerful. Tom goes deeper; he makes us see how strange, how unparalleled, perfect goodness and unlimited power really are, not just among characters from history but even among characters from literature. And then he shows us what that means, its surprising implications for modern "critical" views of the Gospels as legendary or mythical creations.

Again, think about Jesus' teaching in the Sermon on the Mount. Plenty of people will tell you that they think it is fine stuff — a little hard to live up to, but good moral teaching. Tom focuses our attention on what Jesus actually says, which is something none of us could get away with saying. *Who did he think he was?* And then he drives home the point that when Jesus said it, people actually listened to him. That fact, seen in that light, has unexpected consequences. It can help us to answer in a fresh way the more important question: *Who do we think he was?*

This book is full of that kind of insight. The individual pieces are short. You can start almost anywhere. But once you do, if you have (or find yourself developing) an appetite for the questions that really matter, you will probably want to read the whole thing. What you do then will be of more than passing interest to us all.

Introduction

Jesus Christ is too good not to be true.

That's not the usual way you hear that said, I know. I'm not a fan of saying things the usual way. But it does demand explanation, some reason to believe it's true. I'm definitely in favor of that. If there's anything that I've been trying to do on my *Thinking Christian* blog, www.thinkingchristian.net, over these past thirteen years or so, it's to show the great goodness and truth of Jesus Christ, but not in the usual way.

This book comprises the best of my original work curated from *Thinking Christian,* written over the past ten years or so, and chosen for this book because each of them looks at its topic in fresh new ways.

Nothing can be completely new except perhaps certain creative heresies, which I have been careful to avoid. Sometimes, though, insights can come from seeing things in new ways. It can come by noticing connections, for one thing. One of my most life-changing lessons — and one of my three favorite essays in this collection — came from realizing that John the Baptist, famous in Scripture for his humility, said some things that don't sound "humble" at all ("We're Called to be Great").

Sometimes new insights come from noticing what *isn't* there. Another of my favorites in this book, and possibly my most original contribution to worship and apologetics, is based on the fact that Jesus never used his extraordinary powers for his own benefit. He's "Too Good To Be False."

And sometimes – as in "The Map or the Fuel: Living by Grace," which is my third favorite essay here – it's a matter of applying known truths in real life situations. Even there, though, there's a surprising insight from Scripture. I thought "fallen from grace" referred to people who had fallen into obvious sin. Everything changed when I realized that wasn't true.

9

It's these kinds of fresh perspectives that I hope will give you pause throughout this book to say, "That's interesting; I hadn't thought of it that way before!" Which makes my next line ironic, for it's as unoriginal as it gets. I need to say it, though, because it tells why a book like this is so necessary: *The world is growing way more complex, way more challenging, way more difficult to navigate.*

You knew that already. You also know we desperately need fresh thinking in order to keep up with it.

For the Western world has never before seen such a concerted challenge raised up against Christianity as what we're experiencing today. Our brothers and sisters in Asia, North Africa, the Middle East, and certain other troubled spots are familiar with anti-Christian hostility. For us in the West, though — especially in America, which has been mercifully far behind many other countries on this — it's been practically unimaginable, probably even as recently as the day you were born. This monumental change, overturning centuries of precedent, has occurred in your lifetime.

It's just one of many previously unimagined alterations in our landscape. I needn't mention technology. Politics in the U.S. is fairly unrecognizable compared to a few years ago. I could go on, but our heads are spinning fast enough already.

So how does a follower of Christ stay centered, stable, and secure in the midst of the swirling storm? The answer starts in the same place it always has: By holding close to the core, our Rock, Jesus Christ himself, and in the truths he established and communicated to us in his Word. Let the world tilt all it may; he is still our secure foundation.

But that doesn't release us from needing to find our way around all today's unfamiliar spiritual, ethical, and legal challenges. That takes a different kind of centered awareness. We need eyes open, unafraid (in one sense) of what we may see, for we have confidence in Christ whatever comes; yet (in another sense) with appropriate alarm, since harm is still harm.

And we must be quick on our feet. I wonder whether Jesus today might add "nimble as foxes" to "Wise as serpents, innocent as doves;" for those who content themselves with a slow, plodding pace of thought may find themselves answering dated inquiries that have hardly come to anyone's minds in recent years.

Which is why I've tried to keep my thoughts fresh, on the blog and especially in this compendium.

My essays in this book start in Part 1 with Jesus Christ as their main focus. Every apologist I know would say they want to keep Christ in the forefront. Unfortunately, not every apologetics-related book can be — arranged so Christ comes sequentially first — it just doesn't work well for all topics — but this one can be arranged that way, so I'm taking advantage of that to begin with Jesus Christ. Which affords me one further advantage: It allows me to start with less philosophically technical material, and let the challenge ramp up gradually as the book continues.

From the opening essays on Christ, I move on through a series of thoughts on living life in Christ.

Part 2 narrows in on specifics: Though the whole book is intended as an exercise in Christian thinking, this section focuses in on what it actually means to think Christianly, both individually and in community.

Parts 3 through 5 are all in the realm of Christian apologetics. First come three original arguments in favor of the truth of Christianity (Part 3), followed in Part 4 by four essays on the Intelligent Design argument. Just to be sure it's clear: If you're looking for a broad overview either of apologetics or Intelligent Design, you won't find it here, in view of my intention to publish original material instead. You'll want to consult other sources for that.

11

Following that, Part 5 comprises several essays answering atheist and skeptical challenges. They cover confusions regarding the meaning of Christian beliefs in general and the term "faith" in particular, as well as errors that come up when people take up the view called naturalism, meaning roughly that the world is entirely atoms and molecules and physics and math, devoid of any spiritual or supernatural dimension.

The final major section of the book, Part 6, presents works on social and ethical challenges, especially marriage and morality, but also general ethics.

I used to think the most important challenge raised against Christianity was, "It's not true." That's no longer so. Now it's, "Christianity is bad. It's evil. It's unethical." Christianity is (we're told) intolerant, exclusive, and above all homophobic. And if Christians are such a terrible bunch of people, who'd want to join them? That kind of question must be answered, both in Christians' practice and in our thinking.

Part 1: Christ at the Forefront

I open with my favorite topic, Jesus himself, and my cornerstone article, "Too Good to Be False." This article could actually be placed either here in Part 1, "Christ at the Forefront," or in Part 3, on "Positive Apologetics;" for as its title suggests, it presents Jesus' unique character as a powerful reason for believing the accounts couldn't have been faked. It was published in Touchstone magazine's May/June 2014 edition under the title "The Gospel Truth of Jesus." It's used here by permission.

Too Good to Be False

The saying is, "It's too good to be true." Could there be anything or anyone that's too good to be false? I think there is: Jesus Christ himself. If there's one discovery in Christian apologetics I'd want to be remembered for, it's this one, for it starts with the greatness of Jesus and ends with a strong argument against the skeptics' belief that he was just a legend.

"He did not leave us that option: he did not intend to."

Thus C. S. Lewis closes out his famous "Trilemma" argument on the impossibility of Jesus being a great moral teacher and nothing more. The argument is beautiful in its simplicity: it calls for no deep familiarity with New Testament theology or history, only knowledge of the Gospels themselves, and some understanding of human nature. A man claiming to be God, says Lewis, could hardly be good unless he really was God. If Jesus was not the Lord, then (to borrow Josh McDowell's alliterative version of the argument), he must have been a liar or a lunatic.

The questions have changed since Lewis wrote that, though, and it's less common these days to hear Jesus honored as a great moral teacher by those who doubt his deity. Today's skepticism runs deeper than that. The skeptics' line now is that Jesus probably never claimed to be God at all, that the whole story of Jesus, or at least significant portions of it, is nothing more than legend.

Christian apologists have responded with arguments hinging on the correct dates for the composition of the Gospels, the identities of their authors, external corroborating evidence, and the like. All this has been enormously helpful, but one could wish for a more Lewis-like approach to that new L-word, legend — that is, for a way of recognizing the necessary truthfulness of the Gospels from their internal content alone.

15

Lewis was always more at home looking at the evidence of the Gospels themselves than at the historical circumstances surrounding them. In one classic essay (variously titled "Fern-Seed and Elephants" or "Modern Theology and Biblical Criticism," depending on where you find it) he delineates the Gospels as true "reportage" rather than fable, and concludes, "The reader who doesn't see this has simply not learned to read."

It seems to me that the legend hypothesis can be rebutted in a similar way — a way that requires little technical knowledge of the Gospel manuscripts, their dating, and so on, but calls instead for something like Lewis's having "learned to read." As with the original Trilemma, one need only bring to the argument a good working knowledge of the content of the Gospels, particularly as they present the character of Christ, and a clear understanding of human nature — which is where I'll begin my argument.

A Search in Three Questions

Three or four questions concerning human nature have so caught my attention lately that I've taken to asking them of my friends and conference attendees. The first is this: Who are the most powerful characters you can think of in all of human history and imagination, apart from those in the Bible?

The scope of the question is intentionally broad. I exclude biblical personages for reasons that will become clear later, but include everyone else: both historical and quasi-historical figures, as well as characters that are purely the products of human imagination, whether from literature, mythology, film, TV, or even comic books. And I define power in this context as the ability to do and/or obtain whatever one wants without constraint.

The answers I've received range from Andrew Carnegie to Zeus, and include both genuine and doubtful luminaries, such as Genghis Khan, Alexander the Great, Napoleon, Stalin, Mao, and, occasionally, United States presidents. Superman is often mentioned.

My second question is of similar scope, but has a completely different set of characters in mind: Who in all of human history and imagination, outside of the Bible, are the most self-sacrificial, other-oriented, giving, and caring persons you can think of?

The most common answers are Mother Teresa and "my mom." Sir Galahad and Prince Myshkin from Dostoevsky's *The Idiot* have also been suggested, but the set of answers I receive to this question is smaller than to the previous one.

My next question is this: Can you think of any single person — again, outside of the Bible — who genuinely belongs on both lists at the same time? Is there any person in all of human history and imagination who is at the same time supremely powerful and supremely good?

If the second set of answers was small, this one is minuscule. Some of the best suggestions have been Abraham Lincoln, Superman, and Gandalf. Yet none of these characters really measures up as both supremely powerful and supremely other-oriented. Lincoln commanded an army, yes, but his army very nearly lost the Civil War. Gandalf, my own preferred candidate, was entirely dependent on a pair of hobbits, far beyond the reach of his power, for his mission's success. And so far, no one has included him among the most self-sacrificial; his small, weak friends Frodo Baggins and Samwise Gamgee claim that honor above him. Superman remains an interesting case, for reasons I'll specify in a moment.

So, thus far in all my searching, I have not found anyone who's been able to come up with a really satisfying answer to question three. As to why this is, perhaps Abraham Lincoln explained it as succinctly as anyone has: "Nearly all men can stand adversity, but if you want to test a man's character, give him power."

Of course, anyone can just invent a character who is both supremely powerful and supremely self-sacrificial; I can do it in two sentences: Marvin was able to do anything he wanted by his own powers. Marvin did everything for the good of others. But — need I say it? — there's nothing there beyond bald assertion. The challenge is not simply to invent a character and impute to him massive power and towering goodness, but to flesh that character out, to make him interesting and compelling — in short, to make him believable.

Shakespeare never created such a character. Homer didn't either. Dostoevsky never dreamed of such a person. In fact, none of the great poets and writers of any age created a figure who would satisfy question three. I don't know whether that's because they were unable to do so, or because they simply chose not to. But it seems safe to say that, if anyone ever did create such a character and make him believable, that author would have to be counted among the greats, if not as the greatest moral and literary genius of all time.

The Unique Perfection of Christ

And if that is true, and if the character of Christ were created and not rather recorded in the Gospels, then those who created it were those very geniuses. For when we open up the scope of my third question to include biblical characters, the answer comes instantly. Jesus Christ is the one character we can name who is both supremely powerful and supremely self-sacrificial.

Consider his power: Superman can fly through space; Jesus created space. Gandalf can command certain effects with a word; Jesus created everything and upholds it by his word. Lincoln saved his country's unity; Jesus saved all mankind.

There is likewise no comparison between Jesus' sacrifice and anyone else's. Yes, there is a storyline (the Doomsday saga) in which Superman died and was, in a sense, resurrected. Yes, Lincoln could be seen as giving his life in the service of his country. But neither chose his ultimate destiny. Lincoln didn't go to Ford's Theatre that night in order to lay himself down for his country.

18

Kal-el, who became Superman, did not raise his baby hand and volunteer to leave Krypton so he could die to save the earth. Even Gandalf was trying to preserve, not sacrifice, himself when he fell into the chasm during his terrible battle with the Balrog.

Their sacrifices, while real within their contexts, pale beside the sacrifice of Christ, who did it all intentionally from the beginning. As Philippians 2 tells us, Jesus, from before his birth, laid aside the very glory, form, and prerogatives of Godhood, humbling himself to be born in the most helpless of human forms. He came among us as an infant, grew up among us as a boy, and then, once grown to manhood, sacrificed himself for us; and he did it all intentionally — not merely bearing with courage what happened to befall him, but choosing from the start to do what was necessary for our salvation.

Nothing brings the extent of Jesus' self-sacrificial use of power into such clear focus as this question: When did Jesus ever use his supernatural power to benefit himself? Superman used his heat vision to warm up his coffee. Perhaps Jesus drank of the wine at Cana and ate with the throngs for whom he multiplied the loaves and fishes, but he performed those acts for others, not himself. Three times he rebuffed the devil's suggestion that he use his power and position to benefit himself. He walked on water for his own transportation, yes; but did he need to be on that boat for his own purposes? No, he did it because his disciples needed him there.

Not everyone is fully enamored with the morality of Jesus. Some believe he should have more roundly condemned slavery or sexism, for example. Hardly anyone, though, would dispute that he displayed one virtue to a degree unmatched by any other person, whether real or fictional: unconditional, self-sacrificing love.

"The Son of Man did not come to be served but to serve," he said, "and to give his life as a sacrifice for many" (Mark 10:45). This

MAKE SOMEONE 19 ELSE A SUCCESS.

BE ALL CAN BE.

was the consistent pattern of his life, and in it there is both excellence and perfection. By perfection, I mean that there is no flaw in the consistency of the storyline, with respect to Jesus never using his power for his personal benefit.

Let's consider for a moment what this means for Jesus as a literary character. If there is truth in Lord Acton's dictum that absolute power corrupts absolutely, then Jesus, the one possessor of absolute power in all literature, is also the one person who has turned the dictum absolutely upside down. Do not let that wash over you too quickly: it is one case where "absolutely" applies, well, absolutely. Jesus' power was more than just unparalleled; it was absolute. So was his freedom to sacrifice himself or not, a freedom he held from even before his birth. So was his decision to do so.

In short, the man portrayed in the Gospels as the eternal Savior of the whole world must necessarily be a towering figure, as much among literary characters as among historical figures. Jesus Christ is that extraordinary.

A Character of Legend?
The question then arises whether this makes his character more likely to be true, or less likely. Could such a man really have lived among us, or is he more likely the stuff of legend?

Notable among those who adhere to the legend hypothesis are Bart Ehrman, who has written several best-selling books on Christ and the Bible, and the ironically named Reza Aslan, whose best-seller, *Zealot: The Life and Times of Jesus of Nazareth,* just came out last year. These two authors speak with essentially once voice.

Ehrman assures us that his views are representative of many others': they "are not my own idiosyncratic views of the Bible. They are the views that have held sway for many, many years among the majority of serious critical scholars teaching in the universities and seminaries of North America and Europe."

While Ehrman recognizes (along with all other academically credible historians of the New Testament era) that Jesus was a real person, he holds that the most crucial parts of what we understand as the life of Christ never happened. In chapter five of *Jesus, Interrupted,* he takes specific aim at Lewis's trilemma: "I had come to realize," he writes, "that Jesus' divinity was part of John's theology, not a part of Jesus' own teaching ... there were not three options but four: liar, lunatic, Lord, or legend. ... What I meant was that the idea that he called himself God was a legend, which I believe it is."

Legend theories come in many flavors. The highly skeptical Jesus Seminar holds that as much as 85 percent of the Gospels are later accretions upon the life of Jesus Christ. Indeed, it seems that every year some major news magazine comes out with someone's new "historical Jesus." And there are even a small number of self-proclaimed scholars who believe that the entire story of Jesus was made up, that there never was such a person in real life.

Sources of the Legend

But in order for the legend hypothesis to hold water, there must be a plausible explanation for the genesis of the Gospels. Somebody — or more precisely, four somebodies — put the Gospels in writing, and they got their information, or their ideas, from somewhere. And here we encounter a remarkable thing about the story of Christ: that it was placed in its final form not just once but four times, and that each of those four final authors (or author groups) got the crucial aspect of Jesus' character — his perfect power and perfect goodness — exactly right, without flaw.

For the Gospel authors to have produced generally compatible pictures of Jesus would be no surprise: we can certainly assume that they worked interdependently, borrowing sources from each other, relying on common tradition, and so on. In the end, though, they all worked independently to some degree, and yet they all produced a character of unparalleled power and self-sacrifice, with no mar or imperfection of any sort.

The implications of this may be more profound than is commonly recognized. For there seem to be only two plausible explanations for the Gospel writings: either Jesus Christ was a real man, and the Gospel authors painted a consistent picture because they recorded his life faithfully; or he was the stuff of human invention, at least in large part, and all four sources just happened to come up with a character of moral excellence beyond any other in all history or human imagination.

According to the most skeptical scholarship, the character and story of Jesus came about through processes of legendary development. The question is, who would have been involved in that, and what must have been true of them — and is it really likely that they could have accomplished such a feat of moral and literary excellence out of whole cloth? Let's consider what this legend hypothesis calls on us to accept as true.

Non-Communities of Cognitive Dysfunction

First, the legend hypothesis requires us to believe that the Gospels were produced by first- or second-century "communities of faith." Reza Aslan puts it this way in the opening chapter of Zealot:

The Gospels are not, nor were they ever meant to be, historical documentation of Jesus' life. They are not eyewitness accounts of Jesus' words and deeds, recorded by people who knew him. They are testimonies of faith composed by communities of faith and written many years after the events they describe.

This kind of language is typical of legend theorists. Nearly all of them believe that the Gospels were composed by "communities of faith." But this hypothesis, intended to alleviate the Gospels' implausibility, raises its own significant plausibility problems: could the magnificent character of Christ really have bubbled up from a

22

fount of that sort? One gets an uncomfortable feeling, thinking about it: perhaps it's possible, but is it likely? Communities produce stories, yes; one thinks of Till Eulenspiegel, Paul Bunyan, and Pecos Pete. A character like Jesus, however, is of another sort altogether.

Yet that only begins to describe the problem, for legend theorists typically go on to describe what they suppose these authorial communities to have been like, and these added layers of explanation tend to exacerbate the difficulties rather than alleviate them.

The Telephone Game

There is, for example, the "telephone game" version of community-of-faith authorship, a popular theory that has been endorsed by Bart Ehrman, among others. A mainstay of children's birthday parties, the telephone game consists of one child being given a message or story to tell to one other child, who then relays it to a third child, and so on until all the children in sequence have been told the story. As Ehrman notes, usually by the time the last child hears the message, "it's a different story." In Jesus, Interrupted he claims that faith communities came up with and developed their stories of Christ through just this method.

It sounds plausible enough on the surface perhaps —
except that Ehrman emphasizes that this "game" was happening in multiple languages and multiple contexts. Thus, the story was produced by no real community; rather, it came about through dispersed processes of quasi-random serial distortion. By what magic does this loose, far-flung network earn the appellation of "community"?

Genuine communities can create good literature. I've already mentioned Paul Bunyan; growing up in Michigan, I loved reading the folk tales about the great lumberjack and his blue ox, Babe. Communities build and share such stories among each other, through personal, often face-to-face interactions. In such settings, stories grow in parallel processes.

What Ehrman describes is entirely unlike that. It's a serial process, not a parallel one, and the wide assortment of languages, contexts, and cultures involved denotes the very antithesis of community.

A Non-Community of Cognitive Deficiency

Then there is the matter of these stories being developed by communities of faith. Faith, for many skeptics — especially New Atheists — is a form of cognitive deficiency. It is "belief without evidence," or "pretending to know what you don't know." It is a "virus of the mind," an "epistemological illness," say authors like Richard Dawkins, Sam Harris, and Peter Boghossian.

On this view, the authorial source of the Gospels would better be described as a non-community of cognitive deficiency, developing its fables through a "telephone-game" process of ever-multiplying distortion. It seems an unlikely provenance for moral genius in literature.

Each distortion gathered along the way was, of course, another false version of what really happened. Fiction became inextricably mixed into fact. Indeed the fable was spread by the power of its fictions, for its most spectacular — and most erroneous — aspects were what most enticed people into believing it. Its untruths served the purpose of drawing more people to the same untruths. For all we know, some of the fictions were intentional deceptions, at least when first inserted into the fable's creative stream.

This, too, seems to militate against a "community of faith" being the originator of the character of Christ: deceivers, whether intentional or merely careless, are not the stuff of which moral greatness is made.

Clarion Call

There is another theory, however, which relieves the Gospel originators of the charge of intentional deceit. Going under the rubric of cognitive dissonance theory, it lessens the moral severity of the deception, making it not conscious dishonesty, but rather unconscious distortion.

Cognitive dissonance is commonly spoken of, and almost as commonly misunderstood. I first encountered the term as an undergraduate at Michigan State University, in a course on the psychology of social movements. In a fascinating book titled *When Prophecy Fails,* by Leon Festinger and others, we learned the true story of a certain Mrs. Keach (not her real name), who claimed to have received a message from the planet Clarion that the earth would be destroyed on December 21, 1954. Mrs. Keach gathered a group of followers around her whom she convinced would be saved from destruction if they sold everything, quit their jobs, and joined her household.

Their final instruction, for the night of December 20, was to wait obediently in parked cars, from which they would be whisked away by the aliens from Clarion precisely at midnight on the 21st. Midnight arrived on the fateful night; nothing happened. As the hours passed and the aliens still failed to appear, the devotees' eagerness turned to anxiety as they began to wonder if they had given up everything for a lie.

At 4:45 a.m., however, Mrs. Keach relieved them of their distress by relaying a new message from Clarion: the earth had been spared by reason of her followers' sincerity and faithfulness. They had been right all along; indeed, they had saved the world!

Reducing Cognitive Dissonance
It was all utter nonsense, of course, the whole affair a total con. How could Keach's followers have swallowed it so easily? Festinger explained it according to what he called cognitive dissonance reduction theory.

Cognitive dissonance reduction comes into play when individuals have made a significant, active investment of identity and resources in a belief that turns out to be undeniably false: hence the "dissonance" in cognition and the felt need to reduce it.

If just one person has been taken in, he will typically give up the false belief and do his best to live it down. But when a whole group of people have been deceived, they may instead support one another in reducing the cognitive dissonance without giving up the belief. One common means of doing this is for the group to "discover" — i.e., invent — a "fact" showing that they were right all along. Thus, Mrs. Keach's group "learned" that the aliens had decided to spare the earth, and this enabled them to continue believing that the aliens were real and that their investment in that belief had been worth it.

Not surprisingly, this is how some theorists consider the Gospel accounts of the Resurrection to have arisen. Kris Komarnitsky puts it this way: "The belief that Jesus died for our sins and was raised from the dead may have been a way for Jesus' followers to reconcile in their minds his death with their previous hope that he was the Messiah." This rationalization "did not need to be perfect, but it did need to adequately answer what would seem to be the two most natural and pressing questions: why did the Messiah have to die, and how can a dead person be the Messiah?"

Adding Up to a Bad Sum

What these theories add up to is that the surpassingly good and powerful character of Jesus Christ was produced by a community that was no community, expressing the cognitive deficiency called faith through the heavily distorting process of the "telephone game," for the morally dubious purpose of dragging others along into their false belief. Beyond all this (according to some theorists, at least), it was also the product of cognitive meltdown on the same order as believing that waiting overnight in a parked car could bring about the salvation of all mankind.

26

This, or something like it, is supposed to be the description of the authorial source of the one character in all human literature who was perfectly other-centered in spite of holding absolute power: a character expressing moral excellence like no other in all history.

It lacks, if I may say so, the ring of plausibility.

The One Real Option
But if the legend theory is hard to believe, we need another explanation, for the Gospels still came from somewhere and need to be accounted for. The one option we have left is that Jesus Christ was himself the model of perfection whose life and legacy explain the accounts we have in the Gospels. Is this option any more likely than the other?

Both theories can be evaluated according to how they fit with their own back story, how they conform to their conception of reality.

As we have seen, the legend hypothesis presupposes that the world runs on a more or less uniform scale. Anomalies may arise, but they are statistical rarities: Shakespeare and Goethe were outliers. The character of Christ, if it were merely legend, ought at least to have been produced by just such an outlying genius. To ascribe it instead to a non-community of cognitive dysfunction promulgating intentional and/or self-deceiving falsehood is to stretch believability beyond the breaking point. Such a source simply is not one that we could reasonably expect to have produced such a perfect character as Jesus — not even once, much less four times. The legend hypothesis is unreasonable for just that reason.

In contrast, consider the other option's back story. It posits an all-good, all-powerful God, and Jesus as the incarnation of that God. Jesus, the man of perfect moral excellence, fits perfectly in a reality like that. And it also makes sense that those among his apostolic witnesses who were called to record his life would have done so faithfully.

The life of Christ is just too good to be have been produced through legendary processes. It's too good to be false.

And so it seems to me that the "legend" extension of Lewis's Trilemma fails, just as the liar and lunatic ideas fail. I can't help wondering whether Lewis might also have said of the legend hypothesis, "He did not leave us that option: he did not intend to."

Jesus: Who Was He, Really?

Everyone has their view of Jesus. Every religion wants him for their own. That fact in itself argues for his supreme importance in human history. But the religions that "borrow" him for their own use distort his character and everything we know about him.

Can we know the real Jesus? Really?

It's almost embarrassing — yet not the least bit surprising — how many different views of him the world offers. Dallas Willard writes in *The Divine Conspiracy* of one such opinion (p. 134):

> Far too often [Jesus] is regarded as hardly conscious. He is looked on as a mere icon, a wraithlike semblance of a man, fit for the role of sacrificial lamb or alienated social critic, perhaps, but little more. A well-known "scholarly" picture has him wandering the hills of Palestine, deeply confused about who he was and even about crucial points in his basic topic, the kingdom of the heavens. From time to time he perhaps utters disconnected though profound and vaguely radical irrelevancies, now obscurely preserved in our Gospels.

View Upon View

And yet as we survey worldviews and religions, we have view multiplied upon view.

- To many political liberals, and especially to many 20th-century Latin American theologians, Jesus was above all one who came to free the oppressed, often by redistributing wealth but also by showing a new vision of justice.

- To Mennonites, Jesus was a pacifist.

- To Muslims, he was a great prophet.

29

- To followers of the Baha'i faith, he was one of the many prophets, one of many manifestations of God who "have the same metaphysical nature and the same spiritual stature."

- Various cults — Mormons, Jehovah's Witnesses, Unification Church followers, members of "The Way" (now defunct? I haven't heard much of it lately), and others — accord him various levels of high prominence but deny his full unique godhood in the classic Christian sense.

- Whatever sort of unity Unitarian-Universalists may believe in, there is no unity regarding their views of Jesus. Any view seems to be okay; though one Unitarian Universalist pastor once remarked to me that "The resurrection is a goofy doctrine." (My response: that's not the issue. The question is, "Did it happen?")

- New agers likewise have multiple views of Jesus, but tend to emphasize his love, his sensitivity, and above all his non-judgmentalism; and to call on him in support of their belief that everything is going to be just fine for everyone, especially if we could just realize we're all really on the same path after all.

- Secularists consider him an interesting and possibly important historical figure, whose actual significance as an individual, however — if he even existed — has been blown out of all proportion by his followers, many of whom now are rather annoying in their insistence that Jesus really matters.

- And many millions of us believe he is the divine Son of God, Second Person of the Trinity, God with us, the sinless and perfect teacher and example, God's own self-sacrifice for our sins, risen from the dead, now ruling in the heavens and coming back to claim and manifest his rule over all creation; the one who loves all, the one who rescues from sin and death any who will let themselves be so rescued.

- Given half a chance we could go on with even longer descriptions of his greatness and glory.

- Every group has a claim on him. Even 2000 years later, he cannot be ignored. His influence isn't going away. Everyone who knows about him has to make sense of him. This is certainly the reason you find so many versions of Jesus: Everyone wants him on their side.

- In my observations it appears that he gets remade constantly into the image of whoever wants to claim him on their side. He's a conservative or he's a liberal, depending on whether you yourself are conservative or liberal. Is there a way to sort out who he was, really? Is there a way to know the real Jesus, not one molded into our favored version? If there was some such method it would have to meet at least these standards:

- Absolute reliance on the primary sources. We know nothing reliably of him except what is in the Bible, especially the New Testament and a handful of early external sources. Apart from that, every view of Jesus is pure fabrication.

- Attention to context: Jesus lived in a particular setting: a Jew among firmly monotheistic Jews, many of whom gave great credence to their Scriptures, including its prophecies of a Messiah. He lived in a land oppressed by an unwelcome occupying army, where certain religious leaders became his enemies.

- Great care given to guard against making Jesus a member of our own party.

I believe these standards can be satisfactorily met. Among people who take Jesus Christ and the original documents seriously, for example, there are definite cultural and geographical variations. As C.S. Lewis reminded us, these variations cut across time. We have to test our views in relation to each other's views.

Yet it works as Christianity predicts. Philip Jenkins' work in *The Next Christendom* shows that we in the West ought to be learning from Christians in the South and East. In the context of Jesus' own time, most of the above bullet-listed options regarding Jesus are simply impossible. Not to put too fine a point on it, but they

31

are just wrong, and necessarily so. Jesus could not be an impersonal God-force; the Jewish religion and culture would have had none of that sort of thing, and he gave no indication of being that sort of thing.

For the same reason, he could not have been among many "equally valid manifestations" of God. And he couldn't have been a completely non-judgmental teacher of love who only wanted everyone to get along: they wouldn't have killed him for that, would they?

As for the picture Willard presented, wherein some see Jesus as an incompetent, confused, rambling teacher, that hardly seems likely for the founder of the world's largest and most enduring social movement! Who was Jesus, really? I'll go with this, for starters:

He is the Divine Son of God, Second Person of the Trinity, God with us, the sinless and perfect teacher and example, God's own self-sacrifice for our sins, risen from the dead, now ruling in the heavens and coming back to claim and manifest his rule over all creation; the one who loves all, the one who rescues from sin and death any who will let themselves be so rescued.

June 13, 2008

We're Too Used to Jesus

This piece begins abruptly, I'll admit it. It dives right in to saying, "We are too used to Jesus Christ." I suppose I could have softened it with "I feel..." or "Maybe ..." but I'm pretty sure it's really true: We're too used to him. By the end of the essay I hope you'll understand why I say so.

We are too used to Jesus Christ. We miss some of the Bible's most central lessons for it.

Take Matthew 5:17–18, for example. I just looked through more than a dozen top commentaries on those verses. All of them get the theology; all of them miss the stunning reality staring at us in plain view.

The passage reads (ESV):

> Do not think that I have come to abolish the Law or the Prophets; I have not come to abolish them but to fulfill them. For truly, I say to you, until heaven and earth pass away, not an iota, not a dot, will pass from the Law until all is accomplished.

There's a lot to be learned here about the eternal nature of God's law and Jesus' relation to it. It's explained fully in the NT book of Hebrews: Jesus fulfills all the OT worship-law, the ceremonial law by which OT believers pursued their relationship with God. The theology here is really important, and since it gets somewhat complicated, we're used to parsing Jesus' statement here on a purely theological level.

But his listeners weren't cued in on any of that, and they weren't used to Jesus yet. As far as we can tell from the book of Matthew, the crowds of Matt. 7:28 knew little about Jesus, except that he was preaching repentance and the Kingdom of heaven (Matt. 4:17), and that he was a healer (Matt. 4:23–25).

Now he tells them he hasn't come to abolish the Law or the Prophets. Think what's behind that statement. There's a negative point in it: "I haven't come to abolish the Scriptures." Yet there's also a positive statement regarding Jesus' identity implied there.

Only a Nut-Case Would Say That...

We were talking about this at men's Bible study this morning, at a church where I've been a guest preacher. I asked the group, "Suppose I had opened my sermon that day by saying, 'First thing: Please don't think I've come here to abolish the Bible.'"

The guys there reacted instantly, physically, like I'd hit them with a stick. *No one says that.* Why? Because it implies that congregation might actually think that's what you realistically came to do.

No one but a nut-case would open a sermon that way. Cult leaders might try it, but that's part of what makes them nut-cases.

Remember, this was a Jewish crowd. They were already by then the "people of the Book," their devotion to the Law and the Prophets sealed by their history, demonstrated in the accounts of Ezra and Nehemiah, and proved in their devotion to the Temple and the sacrifices. Anyone who came to this crowd with the merest suggestion of abolishing their Bible would have been driven away as a dangerously mad false prophet.

But the crowds listened to Jesus, astonished (Matt. 7:28–29), "for he was teaching them as one who had authority, and not as their scribes." Maybe some people in the crowd were theologically naive, but they still knew their scribes never said, "Well, maybe you think I'm planning to abolish the Bible — and I can see why you might think that — but actually no, don't worry, that isn't not my plan."

Except for the One Who Really Did Have That Authority

Jesus went on to say he was going to fulfill the Law and the Prophets. That's even more audacious. Picture a guest speaker saying, "I'm not actually here to abolish the Bible. I'm here to fulfill everything in it instead." Nut-case time again, unless — and here's the one crucial exception — you're actually the kind of person who can do that.

C.S. Lewis was right: Jesus was no nut-case.[1]

It continues. Jesus gives an entire revolutionary sermon citing absolutely no authority for his teaching except himself. The scribes didn't do that, either. Their teachings would have been footnoted like a modern academic tome with other scholarly sources. Jesus' footnotes would have cited others' teachings only to say they got it wrong and he had it right.

Who did he think he was, anyway?

He believed he was God in the flesh. We can safely believe the same.

Look at Jesus!

Some scholars these days doubt that Jesus saw himself that way. Only God, however, has authority to decide what stays or goes from his Word. Only God has authority to cite no one else but himself as a religious and moral teacher — and later (Matthew 7:21–23) as judge. Only God has authority to say "these words of mine" (Matthew 7:24–27) are the key to each person's final destiny.

The crowds were astonished. We should be, too. Jesus wasn't just teaching theology in that sermon; he was putting himself in the place of God. We shouldn't just look for theology in this sermon:

---

[1]   https://www.goodreads.com/quotes/6979-i-am-trying-here-to-prevent-anyone-saying-the-really

we should look at Jesus himself, and yes, worship him as our God.

And as a closing apologetic footnote I would add this: Does anyone really think this kind of thing could have been made up by a predominantly Jewish community like the early church? Go find out something about first-century Judaism, then try again.

March 23, 2017

Why the Gospels Never Say
Jesus Had Faith

Here's one of those surprising, "how-could-I-have-never-noticed-that-before?" discoveries: The Gospels never say Jesus had faith. How astonishing is that? But there may be a reason for it, and if so, it could be one more sign of his divine nature.

This topic has brought forth controversy and disagreement among Christians whose wisdom and knowledge I trust. Their point is that if Jesus really was made human like us — though also retaining his divine nature — then it would have been necessary for him to exercise faith like us.

There's truth in that, although I still wonder whether his direct knowledge of the Father may have been so different than ours could ever be, the faith he had would have had to be of a different quality or nature, too. So it's an open question in my mind.

If nothing else, it's a new question, a new mystery to ponder: Why don't the Gospels ever mention Jesus having faith?

I was looking over my bookshelf the other day when Fulton Oursler's *The Greatest Faith Ever Known* caught my eye. I've never read it (like too many other books I own), but I know it's about the apostle Paul. And it got me wondering: What about Jesus? Didn't *he* have the greatest faith ever known?

It doesn't look that way, according to the Gospels. Jesus uses the word "faith" 41 times in the Gospels (English Standard Version), and in every case he was speaking of someone else's faith (or lack of it). He never used the term in the first person, speaking of his own faith. Elsewhere in the New Testament, references to Jesus' faith seem different: He is the "author" of faith, it says in Hebrews 12. The nearest thing to an actual statement of Jesus' faith I can find is in 1 Peter 2:23: He "entrusted himself" to the Father. I'll allow that as a legitimate exception to the general statement I'm making.

Contrast that with Paul, who mentioned his own faith at least eighteen times. The one that really stands out in this context is 2 Timothy 3:10: "You, however, have followed my teaching, my conduct, my aim in life, my faith, my patience, my love, my steadfastness...."

Jesus and his followers called on us to follow his teaching, his conduct, his aim in life, his love, and his steadfastness. But unlike his apostle and disciple Paul, he never called on us to model our *faith* after his.

Why It Makes Sense for Him Not to Say He Had Faith
This is striking, to say the least. But there could be a reason for it.

The Bible tells us Jesus is God incarnate. While it might make sense for you or me to speak of having faith in ourselves, it's absurd to think of God as having faith in himself. We talk of faith in ourselves because we know there's reason sometimes to doubt. God knows there is never reason in himself to doubt.

When we trust in God, we trust in another, who has promised to act on our behalf in accord with his character and his promises. Jesus doesn't look to God to act on his behalf.

Yet He Didn't "Lack" Faith
That doesn't mean Jesus lacked faith. There was nothing missing or lacking there.

He had no faith in God, as far as we're told, yet he founded a religion of faith. It was for him the virtue underlying all other virtues, even love, but he didn't explicitly speak of it being one he exemplified. You'd think a religious founder who took a pass on his own chief virtue would be doomed to failure. Not so with Jesus.

A Further Argument for Jesus' Deity

And this could be another argument for the deity of Christ. The only way it makes sense for him not to display faith would be if he was exempt from the need for faith; and the only way any person could be exempt from the need to trust in God would be if that person were God.   *I TRUST IN GOD* *PAST, PRESENT Either to do what he said*

Skeptics say Jesus' deity isn't taught in the first three Gospels *HE SAID* (Matthew, Mark, and Luke), and they question it even in John. I won't go into the several ways they're wrong about what's taught there. My point for today is that they may have missed the importance of what *isn't* taught there. The absence of any mention of Jesus' faith only makes sense if Jesus, unlike all the rest of us, had no need for it: only if he understood himself to be God in the flesh.

December 4, 2014

The Map or The Fuel? Living by Grace

This article was first published in Discipleship Journal *in December 2008. It speaks the heart of Christian freedom like nothing else I've written. Although there's another article that I've said I'd most like to be remembered for ("Too Good to Be False"), this is certainly my most important one on the topic of living the Christian life.*

Fallen from Grace?

It was more than 15 years ago, but I can still remember where I was, alone in my car by the tennis courts in back of a high school in Tustin, California. I was feeling really down on myself, telling myself over and over again, *I'm just not measuring up! I'm just not measuring up!* I had been sincerely trying to live the way I thought a Christian should, but I wasn't succeeding. *What's wrong with me?* I wondered.

My biggest problem, I've realized since then, was that I'd fallen from grace.

"Fallen from grace" isn't a phrase we often apply to Christians who are trying to do their best. Usually it brings to mind a drunk in the gutter or a star executive convicted of fraud and sitting in jail. That's how I used to think of it. I was surprised when I discovered that the Bible uses "fallen from grace" to describe something completely different. The phrase appears in Galatians 5:4 (ESV), where Paul wrote, "You are severed from Christ, you who are seeking to be justified by law; you have fallen away from grace." (The New King James Version says, "you have fallen from grace.")

These Christians were trying to be right with God, but they had the wrong approach. I too was following the wrong approach. I needed a greater understanding of what it means to live by grace. For many believers, living by grace is a difficult concept to grasp.

Yet it is key to experiencing peace and power in our walks with Christ.

Grace vs. Legalism

To understand what it means to live by grace, we first need a clear idea of what grace is and how we access it. Many Christians define grace by the acronym, "God's Riches at Christ's Expense." Grace is indeed God's gift to us. It is God's life, his love, his forgiveness and mercy extended freely to us, based entirely on the merit of Christ, not on our own goodness.

But this gift doesn't come from afar, like mail-order, and it's not a present we open and take away to enjoy on our own. God extends us his grace through a close, living relationship with Christ. To experience His grace, then, we must remain united with Him in a dynamic connection, clinging as closely to him as a branch does to a vine (John 15:1–10).

But that wasn't how the Galatian believers were living. Sure, they were trying so hard to do everything right and follow God's laws. Instead of experiencing closeness to Christ, though, they were "severed from [Him]," said Paul. Really? Where had they gone wrong? It was their trying so hard — and the way they were doing it — that was the problem. They had drifted into *legalism*.

Legalism is the opposite of living by grace. It's based on the belief that one can be justified (attain right standing with God) by following God's rules. Paul addressed this error throughout the book of Galatians, showing in many ways that it's impossible to be right with God by obeying the law. We need grace.

Most evangelical Christians today know enough to avoid the most basic form of this error. We understand our entrance into life in Christ — salvation — comes through faith in Christ alone, and not by keeping God's law. Yet even when our theology of *salvation* is thoroughly grace-based, we can still fall into legalism in *practice*.

41

We should know better. Colossians 2:6–7 tells us that as we have received Christ, we should also walk in Him, rooted and grounded in faith. That is, the way we walk in Christ should be consistent with the way we received him. Many times, though, we fail to extend our understanding of grace and faith past the foundation of *receiving* Christ, to the daily matters of *following* him. We think that we stay right with God by keeping his rules.

That's what the Galatians were doing. After entering a relationship with God through grace, they thought they also needed to obey Jewish laws. But Paul's instruction to them — and all believers — is clear: Just as we receive salvation by faith and grace, not by following rules, we also walk in Christ by faith and grace, not by keeping a list of commands.

The Map or the Fuel?
"But wait a moment!" you say. "The commands in the Bible are there for a reason! Christians must obey these commands!"

Yes, assuredly so. God expects us to do what He tells us. This might seem almost to put us on the cliff of a contradiction: We have commands to obey, but if we seek to be right with God by following them, we are fallen from grace.

So what are we to do? How can we try to heed God's commands and still live by grace? I've puzzled over this dilemma a great deal, and the key seems to lie in where we go to find the strength to carry out God's instructions. We have to make a distinction between the *picture of what is right and the power for doing it*.

God's commands are the *picture*: They describe how God wants us to live. But they can't give us the power, or spiritual strength, to live that way (see Romans 7:2–23). We fall from grace when we begin to look at God's commands, the *picture* of the life he wants for us, to be our *power*.

I did something similar on a trip I took to Wisconsin some time ago. The best flight I could get was to Milwaukee, so had to rent a

42

car to drive to Madison, my final destination. I hadn't been to either city in decades, so I knew nothing about the route; and no one had smart phones in those days, so I gratefully accepted the map the rental car company offered me. In fact, since these maps were free with the rental, I asked for several dozen. I took the maps to the car, opened the gas cap, and stuffed them into the tank one by one.

Well, no, I didn't do that. No one's that stupid! But that's a picture of a law-based approach to obeying God, though. We confuse the map with the fuel: We rely on God's commands to be the fuel to get us to our destination, when in reality, they're just the map of what our destination looks like. In contrast, living by grace means depending on the empowerment we receive through our relationship with Jesus Christ.

Jesus told his disciples,

> Abide in me, and I in you. As the branch cannot bear fruit by itself, unless it abides in the vine, neither can you, unless you abide in me. I am the vine; you are the branches. "Whoever abides in me and I in him, he it is that bears much fruit, for apart from me you can do nothing." (John 15:4,5, ESV)

Elsewhere, Paul tells us to "Walk by the Spirit, and you will not gratify the desires of the flesh" (Galatians 5:16). His word choice reflects the reality that Christ now lives in us in the person of the Holy Spirit. "The fruit of the Spirit," he adds, "is love, joy, peace patience, kindness, goodness, faithfulness, gentleness, self-control…. If we live by the Spirit, let us also walk by the Spirit" (Galatians 5:22–23, 25)

These passages are just a few of many that show us that when we remain in close relationship with Christ through his Spirit, the Spirit will work his fruit in us, and our lives will match the picture shown by the commands. When we're living by grace this way, our life and our strength come from our direct, un-severed connection with Christ, not from focusing on his commands.

43

Still, too often we begin to rely on the rules without realizing it. Wouldn't it be nice if there were alarms to tell us if we're trying to run on the wrong fuel? Actually, there are.

Legalism's Alarm Bells

I've identified several signals in my own life that warn me I'm drifting toward a law-based approach to life:

- Responding to a temptation by telling myself, I shouldn't do that! and hoping such self-talk will enable me to resist. That's the willpower approach to handling sinful desires.

- Trying to motivate myself to do something *"because I should."* That's the duty-based approach to right living

- *Evaluating my standing before God* based on how well I've been following the "shoulds" and the "should nots": If I've kept all the rules on a given day, then I'm OK before God; if I haven't, then I'm not worth much before God that day. That's the performance-based approach to relationship with God.

- *Beating myself up over my sins* because I think my anger will help me do better in the future: *You idiot, Tom! Don't you know that sin didn't do you any good? Just remember how bad you feel now, and let that be a lesson to you next time!* This is the anger-based approach to relationship with God. Certainly we can and should learn from the negative outcomes of our poor decisions. What we should learn, though, is to draw closer to Christ and his unconditional love, not to be harder on ourselves in hopes that will make us do better.

- *Hearing myself say any of these kinds of things* to someone else or paying attention to someone saying it to me.

All these are ways to try to draw power from the rules. When we approach our Christian lives in these ways, we're not relying on relationship with Christ.

44

Grace Under Fire

Need to see how this works in practice? How about when we most need to strengthen our relationship with God: when we're tempted, or even while we're sinning. For example, I'm prone to impatience when I'm on the highway behind a slow driver.

Too often I try to handle this by telling myself, *I shouldn't be* GUILT *feeling so impatient. I shouldn't be muttering at that driver; it* FEAR *isn't the Christian thing to do.* Thoughts like that, filled with "shoulds" and "should nots," are law-based; they have no power to help me. And soon I'm heading right toward road rage.

If you're like me, connecting with Jesus at a time like this is the last thing on your mind. It's terribly humbling to have to admit what's going on inside. Superficial prayers such as, "Lord, help me be patient like I know I ought to be," seem somewhat palatable, but they don't always bring us in close connection to Christ. That comes best by telling God what we're really thinking and feeling.

In fact, that's exactly what I need to do when I'm under temptation, or even when I'm sinning. Anything less is cutting part of myself from Christ, his grace, and his power. The good news is that it's okay: I can really open up toward God in prayer, and it does me good.

That kind of openness might sound something like this: *"Lord, here I am, being tempted to be impatient. What's worse, I think I have a right to be it. I mean, look at all these slow cars in the way. If those jerks just knew how to drive ... and you know what? I really do think they're being jerks. What do you think, Lord?"*

A prayer like that is not pretty. There's rebelliousness being expressed there. But when temptation hits me, when I even slide into sin, praying that way is a genuine move toward abiding in Christ. As I speak to him of my weakness and admit my unruly thoughts, I open my heart toward him so his Spirit can work in me.

CONFESS NOT DENY

45

The closing question in that prayer — "What do you think?" — is crucial. With it I position myself to receive power and direction from the Lord. It's a way of saying, "Jesus, even though I'm a mess, I'm willing to let you do what you want to do in me." *It's in this type of interaction, not in the rules, that I find grace.*

And it's where I find power. God's consistent response to these prayers is to remind me that He accepts me; that I'm a weak, fallen sinner; but that He loves to give me grace. And somehow as He assures me of these truths, the temptation fades. Its strength is broken. Anger and impatience are replaced by God's peace.

Now, if I tried to work up that feeling, all I would experience is the stress of "working up." But by connecting with Christ in my moment of weakness, I experience both peace and victory.

Of course, maintaining closeness with Christ involves more than praying honestly in the midst of temptation. Spending time with him in prayer, in his Word, and with other believes are also important. But it's this kind of moment-by-moment connection with Christ, even in times of testing, that will keep us living by grace and not falling from it.

November 1, 2008

The Dangerous Prayer:
Praying While Sinning

What follows here repeats some of the previous essay. I think it's different enough to help, though.

Temptation
Temptation begins with, "I want to ..."

The second step is, "I shouldn't ..."

The third step is "But I really do want to ..."

The fourth step is what determines the direction of my life, and it's the great difference between Christianity and every other way of living.

Every religion and every secular system recognizes the reality of temptation and wrong-doing. Even in an age of "tolerance" there remain some things everyone knows to be wrong: overeating, throwing the milk carton in the trash instead of recycling it, over-spending, cheating one's customers or employees, letting anger control us, hurting others, and whatever else may have come first to your mind when you realized this article was about temptation. We all face it. We all fail more often than we would like to admit. We all feel bad about it, and we deal with that feeling in different ways.

The Should/Shouldn't Cycle
So what about that fourth step? Here's how it usually goes. *"But I shouldn't!"* Which kicks in a cycle that goes from "I want to" around to "I shouldn't" over and over again. It generally lasts as many times as it takes to get to, *"But I think I will after all."* We don't give in every time, but that's where we end up too often.

47

We battle with ourselves over temptation, and typically we lose. Other people downstream of our sins lose, too.

Christianity offers a completely different fourth step. Too many of us miss it, though; in fact, the apostle Paul wrote to a whole church that was missing it. It was a group of Christians in Galatia who kept on trying to do the right thing by concentrating on "the works of the law" — which is another way of saying they were focusing on the rules: "I should do this, I should never do that."

Paul excoriated them for it. "You foolish Galatians," he wrote in Galatians 3:1, "who has bewitched you?" Later he told them they had "fallen from grace" (Gal. 5:4, NKJV). I'll bet you thought "fallen from grace" was a label for pastors and governors who got caught with mistresses. But no.

How the Christian Answer Is Different

God isn't just an after-the-fact repair-man, you see. He gave us the gift of himself, dwelling with us and in us through the third Person of the Trinity, the Holy Spirit, often called the Spirit of Christ. That's what makes Christianity different in the moment of temptation. I'll explain by referring back to the Gal. 5:4 verse I mentioned earlier. Paul said there that the problem with these Christians who were trying really hard to do right, these *foolish, bewitched* Christians who were trying to do right (imagine that!), was that they were *severed from Christ.* Obviously, that's wrong; obviously we are to be connected to Christ instead (Christ himself speaks of this, especially in John 15).

Which makes all the difference when we're experiencing tempta-tion. Suppose you're in the third step: "But I really do want to ..." Here's how it might go from there as you remain connected with Christ. Instead of trying to argue yourself out of giving in to the sin, you can say, *"Let's be honest. I really do want to give in to this temptation... and I also want to be connected to Christ. So right now, I invite Christ to be with me in this moment, even while*

48

I'm at the point of really wanting to do something he wouldn't like."

Praying While Sinning

Do you see how that breaks the cycle of "I want to — I shouldn't — but I want to — but I shouldn't"? It's not just a psychological trick. It's inviting the real goodness and power of God into the cycle. I experienced the result again just this morning: Instead of fighting through the cycle, I found myself reflecting on God's goodness, enjoying his company, and almost forgetting about the wrong thing that had seemed so powerfully motivating just moments earlier. The temptation evaporated. I didn't fight it off. God did.

But what if you've gone beyond that third step? What if you've given in to the sin, and you're right in the middle of it? *What if you're even enjoying it?* Sin can be pretty fun for a while, after all. It wouldn't be tempting if it weren't!

Even then it's not too late to draw Christ in, though. It's the right time for what I call the "dangerous prayer." This prayer is honest, it's open, it's prayed right in the middle of sinning, and it brings Christ right there with you in the midst of it.

It goes something like this: "Lord Christ, I know this is wrong, but I'm actually having a good time at the moment. Would you come and be with me here right now while I'm being tempted or while I'm sinning? And would you let me know what you think about it while you're here?"

Can we pray that way? I believe we have to. I'm a great believer in praying while sinning. (I do *not* believe in sinning while praying!) God is not shocked to learn we're sinning, and he's not surprised to discover we're having a moment of passing fun with it. He's there anyway, and he loves us no less then, that at any other time.

49

What this prayer does, then, is to wake us up to his presence, and make us open to his work in our hearts. In return God wakes us up to reality, so we can see the truth about how weak and transitory that sinful pleasure really is. I've found that when I pray that way, typically I can walk away from the sin with hardly any struggle. Christ does the fighting for me! He's the rescuer from sin, after all. I call on him to come in with me so he can draw me out.

Honest with Self and with God

You see, if resisting temptation means telling myself, "I shouldn't want this!" it's destined to fail, because temptation means I *do* want this, or at least I think I do at this moment. If standing up against sin means trying to think of something else I want more ("I'd rather be thin than eat this piece of cake"), that has a bit more power — but darn it, that cake still looks awfully good, and I'm not really all that sure how *being thin next month* stacks up against *that cake right there right now*.

But if we can say, "You know I really do want this thing that's tempting me, and I'm going to invite someone to be with me," that's not denying anything that's true about ourselves. And if that person is the One with all spiritual power and righteousness, then we have an incredible ally on our side.

There is more on this later in the book of Galatians, where Paul talks about the Holy Spirit, the third Person of the Trinity, as the real and powerful living presence of God in Christians. "Walk by the Spirit," he says, "and you will not fulfill the desires of the flesh" (Galatians 5:16).

Relationship, Not Rules

That's what makes Christianity different. It's a relationship, not a set of rules. I'm not saying the rules don't matter, for they show us a picture of what it is to do right, but there's no real power in the act of scrunching up our willpower to follow the rules. The power comes through Christ in us. We need to be careful that our relationship is with the genuine person of Christ, too, which is one reason among many for staying in the Scriptures and in fellowship with other believers. Scripture keeps us in touch with the real Christ, and other believers can help keep us from getting goofy ideas about both God and sin.

Christianity is different from every other religion and every other secular system. Every other system says it's up to us to get right with God, the world, or ourselves. No other system has real power to break the temptation-desire-sin cycle the way Christ does. No other system includes such a powerful personal relationship at its core. No other system can rescue us in the moment the way Christ himself can.

So whether you're already a believer or just checking out this strange phenomenon of a "thinking Christian," I hope that sounds attractive to you, because it really is good.

If you're already a believer, I hope you'll pray the dangerous prayer, and discover the power Christ has to come in and bring you out. If you're not yet a believer, but you've experienced the pain of personal failure (as we all have), I hope you'll give Jesus Christ a try.

September 30, 2011

The Humbling Insult of God's Unconditional Love

The title of this piece is provocative — intentionally so. The word "insult" doesn't seem to fit when we think of God's love for us, and it doesn't — provided we accept it in true humility. Otherwise, though, it really is likely to feel insulting. Here's why.

It takes humility to accept God's love. Why? Because we can't earn it. Not even close.

Not that we don't do all we can to try. Christianity's chief heresy through the ages has been legalism: seeking to earn favor with God by what we do. It's a Christian fault just because it's a very human fault.

We don't just want to be loved; we want to be good enough to be loved. With God, we want to be the sort of thing that could *earn* his love. We want to show that we deserve it, that he owes it to us for the special things we do. The fact is, we really are worthy of his love, but not by our own works or goodness. We are worthy because he has deemed us so. *GoD SAYS So*

But that's hardly satisfying to us who want to be able to show we're good enough. So we dream up doctrines that say that our works will make us worthy. They won't. We can do nothing — zero! — to make ourselves worthy before God. God loves us anyway, but some of us have trouble with that. I think that might be — though it's dangerous to say — because there is something of a paradoxical insult in the way God loves us.

If we could stand before him, you see, and tell him, "Thank you very much, God, for your love; and of course everyone can certainly see what I've done to earn it" — if we could only say that,

52

now *that* would be something to be proud of. We could really feel good about ourselves!

But that's not how it is. For us to be able to face God that way, he would have to be shrunk down to our size. He would no longer be the object of our worship, but the subject of our manipulation.

Legalism as Manipulation

And I think to a great extent that's actually what legalism is about. It's about manipulating God, trying to get on his good side, so that we can get good things from him or feel good and special about ourselves. Even a teenager, though, can sense manipulation a mile away. How much more do you suppose God sees it and resists it?

"THAT I WAS LIKE YOU"

Yet here's the astonishing thing: We try to shrink God to our size so we can impress him — and how God must laugh at that! — and yet he emptied *himself,* and in a sense shrunk himself down to our size. He was born a babe in a stable, grew up in a craftsman's home, wandered for a few years and taught a small band of followers. In the course of all this he met two kinds of responses. Some people insisted on being impressive before him. He defeated them both by argument and by his works. Some, however, saw the grandeur of God in him, and he set them on a course toward a Kingdom.

And still today, it is those who humble themselves before him who will be lifted up.

The Humility of Being Loved

For many of us, the hardest part of all this is knowing it's his own goodness, not ours, that motivates God to love us. We need not earn it; we never *could* earn it; but for those who want real love, it's there in abundance, without measure. It comes with just one condition: that we accept it on his terms, not on our own.

Humbled? Insulted, even? Then you get the point. Looking for God's love anyway? Then bear the insult, if it seems that way to

53

you, look to him for his goodness, and enjoy his unconditional favor. He gives it to show his own goodness, not to make us look
good. Thank God, though — he gives it!

May 23, 2008

SH&O HIS LOUE.

Don't Pray for Patience

We pray for patience, but we do it with fear that God will really answer. He'll put us through hard training to learn it. Or at least how I've heard people talk about it. I think there's a better way to pray, though, based on knowing what Christian patience is really all about.

Have you heard this one? "Don't pray for God to teach you patience — you won't like what he'll put you through to learn it!"

I don't think much of that reasoning. It makes God look like a nasty schoolmaster, for one thing. It's also the wrong reason. That is, I agree with the advice, "Don't pray for patience." I just think there's a far better reason for it.

Lessons from experience
I think I have a bit of background from which to speak about this. For six years I've been unable to walk without pain and a limp. Repeatedly, through probably half of those years the doctors and therapists told me I'm about six to eight weeks from full recovery.

Obviously, it's turned out to be a lot more complicated than that — five surgeries' worth, actually. Obviously, too, I waited for that recovery, which remained firmly and consistently just out of sight around the corner. It would have been easier just to have known how long it was going to take from the start, instead of dealing with the repeated disappointment of unsuccessful treatments all this time.

The first surgery was kind of a pain, and the second and third and fourth were disappointing, but I made it through in pretty good spiritual and emotional condition. The latest one has been really rough, though. I've had real trouble pushing through the emotional barriers: the pain, the fatigue, the effects of lost sleep, and the discouragement that's been lurking at the edge of my consciousness and sometimes pushing its way right in. I'm tired, I'm feeling a lot of loss, and I'm simply feeling sad a lot of the time.

Patience? So what?

Here's another way to look at what I just said. I did fine with all this, emotionally and spiritually, for a long time. That was patience in action. I would go so far as to say it shows I practiced patience to a fairly high degree. Which might mean I'd even *learned* patience to a high degree. Sure, I could use more of it in traffic, and sometimes also in conversation with my family members (okay, not just *sometimes),* but still most people would agree, I'm no slouch at this patience thing.

But so what? *Why does patience matter? What's it good for?* It's a mark of a mature character, one might say. So again, *why does that matter?*

God didn't create us to be great at toughing things out

I was thinking about all these things earlier today — a lot earlier, in fact, at about 3:15 or 3:30 this morning, when I would rather have been sleeping. It was worth being awake this time, though, because that's when I realized that patience wasn't the point. God didn't create me to become great at toughing things out. He created me as someone to love. He created me to love him. And he created me to live in loving relationship with others.

Yes, Scripture speaks often about growing in patience, learning endurance, and so on — but patience itself isn't the point. Rather, patience reflects our trust in God, and it supports our relationship with others.

Patience is for relationships

It's not hard to see how patience supports our relationships with others. Look, if everyone would just do what I want them to do, the way I want and when I want, I'd never need to be patient with them. Conversely, however, if I would quit harboring the desire that they would be that way, they'd have a lot less need for patience with me!

Impatient relationships are self-centered relationships. I'm not loving you if I expect you to operate on my agenda and my schedule.

When it comes to relationships, love is the point. The apostle Paul didn't write, "and now abide faith, hope, and patience, these three; but the greatest of these is patience." He identified love as the greatest virtue (1 Cor. 13:13). Patience counts interpersonally precisely because it is a way of loving.

Patience is the emotional fruit of trust in God

In relationship with God, patience is a way of trusting. This is what really struck me while lying awake this morning. Impatience is a way of telling God I don't think he's doing his job right. It's an expression of distrust toward God's wisdom, his goodness, and his timing.

I distinguish impatience from dissatisfaction, which I can illustrate again with the story of my foot. I can be dissatisfied with its current atrophied condition, and I can let that drive me to do the physical therapy I've been prescribed, while trusting God to be loving me and doing good for me regardless of my physical condition. Or to look at it on another scale, my dissatisfaction with the state of the world can drive me to pitch in and do my part to help.

The difference between godly patience and ungodly impatience isn't (as some might think) that patience waits while impatience acts. Patience could be very quiet or very active; either one is possible. Either way, patience trusts God to be taking care of me today and my work's outcome tomorrow — or my prayers' outcome, or my relationship efforts' outcome, or my waiting's outcome.

What that really means, then, is that patience is the emotional fruit of active trust in God's goodness and love.

So early this morning, while lying in bed, I told God, *This is a really long road you're asking me to walk (or limp) along. Right now I want to tell you I love you, and I'm going to quiet my heart and let you love me.*

Don't pray for patience, pray for love and trust instead.
That's why I don't think patience is the point. Love and trust are. Patience matters, yes, but it matters because it is an expression — and an observable measure — of what really counts: my love and my trust.

That's why I don't think much of the usual advice about praying for patience. My advice instead would be, *Don't pray for God to teach you patience. Pray that he would teach you to love more and trust more.*

September 23, 2015

The Truth Holds Us

"The truth holds us" has been my blog's tagline, off and on, from the beginning. It's my best answer to the charge that Christians are annoyingly arrogant for thinking we hold the truth. I agree it's true: If we think we hold the truth, we really are arrogant. It's actually the other way around: The Truth holds us.

It's awkward being a Christian these days. We claim to know the truth about God, morality, and a host of other contested things. We believe this truth is unique and applies to all people for all time. We believe that where other so-called truths contradict the one we hold to, those other "truths" are wrong, and ours is right. We believe that the truth is so tied together with Jesus Christ that he could claim, "I am the truth."

For many people, that's nothing but arrogance in action. "Who are you to claim you've got the one truth for everyone? Some things in mathematics might be true for everyone and for all time, but that's about all. Scientists know how often the 'truths' of one age are later corrected or replaced. To claim you have the truth in morality and religion is arrogant, unaware, and intolerant. It's just plain *wrong.*"

A Humble Approach to Truth

And indeed, if we really thought *our* truth was true for everyone, we really would be arrogant. But the truth is exactly the opposite. When we say, "I know the truth," we're not claiming superiority, we're taking a position of humility, even though that's not the way it looks.

You won't understand this, though, without considering it in light of how people understand truth. It's common today for people to develop what they consider their own personal truths regarding religion and ethics. They build their truths to fit themselves, to

59

make sense for themselves. These "truths" are *personal* truths. But Christians don't see it that way at all. Our truth is not our own; it's not personal truth. It's never been ours to create or build for ourselves; it's a reality to be discovered. It's truth that holds true whether we like it or not. Christians do not own the truth; we submit to it.

Which Is More Arrogant?

And which is more arrogant: to think we can build our own personal truth, or to submit humbly to one that's bigger than ourselves? Consider C.S. Lewis. A firm atheist, he was at Oxford when he decided to study the evidence regarding God. It led him in a direction he did not choose:

> You must picture me alone in [my] room... night after night, feeling, whenever my mind lifted even for a second from my work, the steady, unrelenting approach of Him whom I so earnestly desired not to meet... That which I greatly feared had at last come upon me... I gave in and admitted that God was God and knelt and prayed: perhaps, that night the most dejected and reluctant convert in all England.

There was no arrogance in that. There was giving in and admitting. He submitted to something greater than himself.

We Don't Hold the Truth, the Truth Holds Us

Contrast that with the idea that we can all develop our own truth. Isn't that awfully bold? Isn't it spitting in the face of reality? Isn't that like saying, "Hey, Reality, step aside! It's up to me to decide what's true and what isn't!" Who's being arrogant here? Christians know that we are constrained by reality. Though we don't always put it this way, we don't believe we hold the truth. We believe *the truth holds us*.

It would be so simple to ride with the flow of the age, to relax and let go of issues such as abortion, gay marriage, sexual freedom and so on. We can't. If we bow before the truth, we must be led by it, even if it leads us into unpopular territory. "But you must

60

have an open mind!" say some. Another sparkling writer of the 20th century, G.K. Chesterton, answered this way: "The point of having an open mind, like having an open mouth, is to close it on something solid."

I have spent hours studying viewpoints contrary to Christianity. I continue to find that God's word is solid and nourishing, and ultimately makes more sense than the alternatives. The truth holds me. As Martin Luther said (or was reported to say, at least), *"Hier stehe ich. Ich kann nicht anders."* ("Here I stand, I can do no other.")

Recognizing What We Know and Don't Know

Honestly, I wish the truth held me more. Any Christian would be deceitful to pretend he or she practices it fully, even as far as he or she understands it. It would be just as bad to say we grasp it all. Even the simple commands, to love God fully and to love our neighbor as ourselves, have a depth beyond reaching.

Many aspects of the faith are clear enough, for instance, the basics: that Jesus claimed to be God in the flesh and supported his claim by his life, death, and resurrection. But there are other sides of Christianity that remain mysterious or difficult. Our age has come up with new questions (genetic engineering, genocide, end-of-life decisions, and global environmental issues, for example) that require us to work out anew how God's word applies. This, too, is reason for humility.

Misplaced Humility

I'm reminded again of Chesterton at this point, though:

> What we suffer from today is humility in the wrong place. Modesty has moved from the organ of ambition. Modesty has settled upon the organ of conviction; where it was never meant to be. A man was meant to be doubtful about himself, but undoubting about the truth; this has been exactly reversed. Nowadays the part of a man that a man does assert is

exactly the part he ought not to assert – himself. The part he doubts is exactly the part he ought not to doubt – the Divine Reason.

He's encouraging believers to be confident of the truth we know.

A Very Good Truth

Now if we're *submitting* to the truth, does that mean we're stuck in some dark corner where there's no freedom to move? Not at all! C.S. Lewis also wrote of Joy (he always capitalized it) that led him toward Christ and flowed out of his relationship with God. The truth in Christ is not a cold, abstract principle, but a person of infinite love and grace.

The Bible tells us to "speak the truth in love," and clearly implies that it should generally be accompanied with a smile. Those who deny there is such a thing as truth may find it hard to see that smile. We're offering it. It's not a smile that says, "Whatever you do, whatever you believe, is fine," for that would be a denial of the truth — Jesus Christ — who is also love.

Instead it's an invitation to encounter reality for what it truly is. For it is what it is, not what anyone makes it up to be. And it is a very good reality we're inviting you to see, to acknowledge, and to enter into. We're inviting you to let go of your made-up "truths," and let this real truth, this *good* truth, hold you.

August 25, 2009

How "Jesus Saves" Makes So Much More Sense than "Jesus Approves"

I get the sense sometimes that liberal-leaning Christians want to tell us how much Jesus approves of everyone. That's a nice, kind thought, but it makes no sense of human nature, and it makes no sense of Jesus.

Once upon a time, people everywhere knew what it meant that "Jesus saves." Punsters would add, "at First National Bank," but the joke doesn't work anymore. In most of Western culture now, neither the biblical phrase nor the pun is heard much. The concept now (if not the wording) is *Jesus approves.*

"Jesus saves" is a forgotten conception. It certainly needs explanation in our day. Some people have taken to saying "Jesus rescues" instead; or "Jesus is our forgiver." But the original phrase (original in English, at least) is still valid, if only we could get the point across. It's definitely more accurate than "Jesus approves."

And it's also a whole lot more interesting. It's a strong enough conception to explain the world's fascination with Jesus lasting through two millennia, across every part of the world. A historical figure who merely *approved* could never have gained such a compelling hold upon humanity.

But let's pause for a look at this idea of Jesus as the one who approves. Lots of people are saying it.

"Jesus-Who-Approves"
Former President Jimmy Carter is one:

> "I believe Jesus would approve gay marriage, but that's just my own personal belief," the Democrat said in an interview on HuffPost Live. "I think Jesus would encourage any love

affair if it was honest and sincere and was not damaging to anyone else, and I don't see that gay marriage damages anyone else," he added.[2]

Julie LaBrecque, commenting at allenbwest.com, wrote,

> Who am I to judge? If Christianity is valid, don't you think Jesus would advocate inclusiveness, diversity, tolerance and love and respect for our fellow humans? Jesus in the Gospels says nothing about homosexuality. It is the hyper-moralist, St. Paul, who mucked things up and turned the simple teachings of Jesus into some intolerant and cruel [un-Christian] judgmentalism. I prefer Jesus to Paul and science to fantasy.[3]

A. J. Walton, the self-styled "Idealist, Advocate, Hopeful Urban Sophisticate" at Huffington Post, quoting a gay pride poster saying, "God Thinks You're Absolutely Fabulous," put it this way:

Joel Osteen

> That's what made my first Pride March so holy. There I stood, a young LGBT man and student of theology whose task was to convey God's love and affirmation of same-sex love to people of faith and no faith.[4]

It Doesn't Fit the Picture

And the classic rock song went, "Jesus is just alright with me." What the Doobie Brothers might have meant there (viewing it charitably) was that they were willing to side with Jesus. Now, though it's more like, "Whatever I want to be, Jesus is alright with it. He's here to approve!"

---

2   thehill.com/blogs/blog-briefing-room/news/247068-jimmy-carter-jesus-would-approve-gay-marriage
3   https://www.allenwest.com/2015/06/26/why-the-supreme-court-ruling-on-gay-marriage-could-lead-to-civil-war/
4   https://www.huffingtonpost.com/aj-walton/god-thinks-youre-absolutely-fabulous_b_7971222.html_

But this makes hardly any historical sense. How likely is it that one who just went around approving people's preferences would have so captured the world? Doesn't it seem it would have taken a stronger character than that?

Jesus-who-approves is a flat character, not even two-dimensional. Flat characters do not leave lasting influence.

The real Jesus, in contrast, stands as a towering figure in history. It isn't because he bent to others' whims. It's because he effectively forced history's view of true character to bend to his character rather than vice versa. He showed how love could be far more just, true, sacrificial, and by the way, more interesting and complex than mere approval.

It took a person of real substance to change the world the way Jesus did. It took someone with an absolutely solid grip on moral and spiritual realities — the levers that lift and turn a world. Jesus had that. It took someone whose love went leagues deep to motivate people to follow him. It took total mastery of the human condition. It took all this wrapped up in one person to be a world-changer across the millennia.

Anything less than that, and no one would have ever found him interesting. Yet they did then, and billions still do today. Jesus who saves is far more real, more substantial, more historically likely, more believable, than Jesus who merely approves.

Jesus-Who-Approves Isn't the Real Jesus
And Jesus-who-approves is a made-up character anyway.

There is a "Jesus" who approves of whatever moral novelty *we* think he would approve, and there is Jesus as he's recorded in the Gospel accounts. The two versions of Jesus could hardly be more different.

Jesus-who-approves is a Jesus of grace, who accepts sinners as they are, who dined in their homes, who even partied with them.

65

Which is accurate — so far. The problem is, it's only half-true. Which makes it a false picture of him after all.

John 1:14 tells us he came in both grace and truth. The truth he came with was that God invites us as we are, but not so we can stay that way. God calls *us*, not our sin, to himself. Our sin actually presents a huge barrier between God and us. God will accept us as we are, but only because Jesus paid the high price by which the barrier could be broken, and we could be reconciled to God.

So yes, Jesus says *you and I* can be okay in relation to God; but he never said *sin* could be. To the woman taken in adultery (John 8:1–12) he said in all grace, "Neither do I condemn you." Then he added, "Go and sin no more."

August 13, 2015

GRACE = TRUTH

Christianity Is No Crutch — And I Should Know

Ever heard the line, "Christianity is just a crutch for weak people who can't make it on their own"? I've got some pretty strong opinions on that one, based on way too much personal experience.

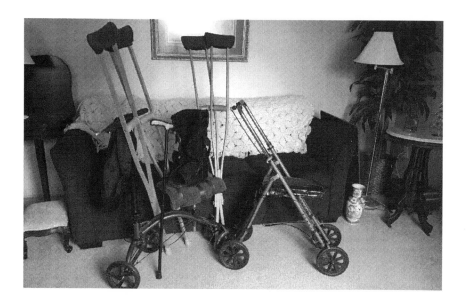

Have you heard this one?

"Christianity is just a crutch for people who don't have the strength to make it on their own."

Maybe you've even said it yourself. Here's my short answer: No, Christianity is nothing like a crutch. Not even close. And I should know

Knowing Crutches
I think I can safely say I know something about crutches.

I was born with an extra bone in each foot, and it's caused no end of trouble. The photo above shows my current collection: two sets of crutches (one pair stays in the car, just in case); two knee walkers (different models suited for different terrain); one cane, and my current orthopedic boot.

Not shown: the five or six casts I've worn, the three previous boots I've worn out and thrown away, and the worn-down brakes on both knee walkers from the miles I've driven them. Also not shown are all the compression stockings, Ace bandages, ice packs, and physical therapy equipment I use regularly.

This has been going on for pretty much all of the past five years, and a large portion of the fifteen years preceding that.

There's No Analogy There
I know a little bit about following Christ, too, after almost 42 years of experience. And what I know is that Christianity has virtually nothing in common with crutches; in fact, it's infinitely beyond compare.

Sure, life can be hard. Sometimes you need help making it through. But that's far, far, *far* from the whole reason it's good to be in a relationship with Christ.

Additionally, yes, we're all destined to die in our sin without Christ, but that doesn't make him merely a crutch to keep us going.

I used to get that last point wrong. I used to say, "No, Christianity isn't a crutch. It's more like an iron lung: without it you can't even live!" There's some truth in that: you can't live without Christ. But there's an awful lot that's wrong, too. Living in Christ is freeing, not confining; it's joyful, not something to endure.

Not only that, but an iron lung is a medical device that keeps the living from dying. Christianity, in complete contrast, is a relationship that revives the spiritually dead to true life. An iron lung sustains a nearly-expiring life; Jesus Christ creates a brand-new life.

So I'll never use that analogy again. I wish I could go back and correct it with everyone I ever said it to.

Knowing Christ!

What about crutches, though? Again, there's no comparison. For all the hundreds of times I've picked up a pair of crutches, I've never once felt the same thing I do when I pray or read the Bible or worship with other Christians. With crutches I never feel, *This is so good! This is so life-giving! This is so right and true!* But consistently that's my experience when I encounter God through Jesus Christ.

The atheist or skeptic may retort, "You're using your emotions to make a case for your religion, and that's not valid." I have a two-part answer to that.

First, we all know that what they mean is Christianity is an *emotional* crutch. Since they've brought up feelings, it's rationally legitimate for me to tell them about feelings in my response.

But the second part of my answer is what I really want to camp on. I want everyone to know that following Jesus Christ, living in a personal relationship with Him, is *great!* It's life-giving! It's a life filled with strength: strength that flows inside and builds you up, while also supporting you from the outside. It's filled with love.

Be Strong in Grace Time

I have never said, "Wow, I love to be on crutches!" But I have often said, "It is so good to able to sit down and pray right now!" I haven't experienced prayer that way every time, but I've felt that kind of joy *infinitely* more with approaching God than I ever have with crutches. Again: there's no comparison there. None.

69

It Isn't Just About "Comfort," Either

Here's a related point you've probably also run across: "Faith is fine if you need that kind of comfort." I'll admit: I need comfort. You don't go through repeated disabilities without needing it. This latest round has been especially hard. My wife will tell you I haven't always connected with God to get the strength I need from Him.

But when I do draw close to God, what I experience is nothing like mere comfort: "There, there, you're going to be okay." It's much more like, "Stand tall, Tom! I'm pouring my power and love straight into your soul, so you can have strength and joy even if things aren't 'okay.'"

Not Just "Good When You Need It"

Here's another difference. Crutches and the orthopedic boot never feel right, but there are times when they feel good. That's when I know something's wrong for sure. If using those aids feels good, it means I've got a problem and it needs relief. I would never use them when I'm healthy; they would feel obviously wrong and in the way.

Relating to God isn't like that. It's good when I need him most, no doubt about that. It's good when I'm doing fine, too. I don't appreciate him just for rescuing me when I need relief from some problem. I can enjoy fellowship with him at any time, and I do.

It's About an Abundantly Full New Life

Anyone who says Christianity is just a crutch, or faith is mere comfort, either doesn't know crutches or doesn't know Christianity. There's no comparison there.

In fact, I'm not sure what to compare it to. Think of it as the difference between the dead of winter and the new life of spring; or the joy of your favorite activity (swimming or canoeing for me) versus the dread of lying sick in the hospital. It's that much better.

Following Jesus Christ isn't about making it through. It's about relishing the abundantly full new life he gives.

December 9, 2016

If Christianity is Your Religion, Don't Thank God for the Cross

If you're reading these essays in order, you've already discovered I like provocative titles. I start this piece with a provocative first paragraph, too. The point here, though, is to remember whose religion Christianity is. We didn't come up with it. It isn't our religion.

If Christianity were my religion, I wouldn't thank God for the Cross. But it's not my religion, and on Thanksgiving Day here in the U.S. tomorrow, I will be giving God all the thanks I can give him for the Cross of Jesus Christ.

I know I need to explain that, and I will. It starts with what I mean when I say, "my religion." Because that makes all the difference.

Choosing Our Religions

We live in a world of religious pluralism. A recent Gallup poll says that 70 percent of North Americans believe that many religious could lead you to God. The Pew Forum surveyed Americans who belong to various religions in 2008. They found that 57 percent of Americans who attend Bible-believing churches (evangelical or black churches, in their study) believe that many religions can lead to God.

I take it that most of those 57% believe their choice of Christianity is an expression of their personal preference. Maybe it has to do with their culture, upbringing, friends in church, or what they're comfortable with. As far as spiritual life goes, though, they think they have a choice, and the choice they've made is evangelical Christianity. They picked it out, and it's their religion.

For my part, I follow Jesus Christ and his teachings, to the best of my capacity in Christ. I am a Christian. I do not, however, consider Christianity my chosen religion. I didn't pick it off some religious clothes rack; I didn't say, "I don't really feel like a Buddhist or a Muslim for this life; I'm a traditional American, so the Christian thing just seems to fit me better."

I didn't buy it and I'm not trying to make it my own. Christianity is too big, too grand, too filled with God for that. I am a Christian because the one God has called me to relate to him in that unique way. If Christianity were my choice from a list of options, if it were my religion in that sense, I wouldn't thank God for the cross.

History's Most Despicable Act of Injustice?
After all, how could I thank God for it? Remember how at Gethsemane Jesus prayed that this cup could pass from him? He was asking the Father (though he knew the answer already), "Couldn't there be some other way?!" He was arrested in humiliation and betrayal. Couldn't that have been avoided? He was humiliated in trials before the Jewish court, Pilate, and Herod.

Did he really have to go through that? He was mocked, beaten, tortured. Was that really necessary? He was hung on the Cross until he screamed the agony of forsakenness; and he died. Why, God? WHY?

Why? Because he loved us and wanted to bring us to God, and because there was *no other way*. Think about it: What if there had been another way? What if the 57 percent believe correctly that Christianity is one of many true ways to God? Then the Cross should never have happened. The cup should have passed from the hand of the Son of God. There would have been no need for his brutal passion experience.

Far from being something to thank God for, the Cross would have been the worst of all needless atrocities in history.

73

So do not — I repeat, do not! — say, "All religions lead to God, but since I've grown up a Christian, I'll follow that path for myself." Do not make Christianity your religion that way. If you do, it is as if you are glorifying history's most despicable act of cosmic cruelty. If you think there are multiple paths to God, then for Christ's sake (I mean that reverently and literally), don't choose Christianity! Don't choose the religion that includes his torture and execution! *No other way!*

Or History's Most Astonishing Declaration of Love and Justice

The question, you see, hinges on *whether Jesus really did die on the cross for our sins,* the just for the unjust, that he might bring us to God. If he did, then we can be sure he did it because it was the only way to God. He said so himself in John 14:6. I am convinced that he did; that the God who created us entered human history in the form of a child who grew to be a man; who taught, healed, and demonstrated a life given wholly to God; and who died on the Cross, was raised from the dead, and was glorified into heaven.

I am convinced he did it because it was the only way we could come to God. He did it for love; for the joy set before him, knowing the life it brings to us whom he loves. He was willing to endure it because it was necessary in order to reconcile humans to God. The Cross was good, but it was only good because it was the only good way to bring us to God.

So I do not follow Christ because Christianity is my religion of choice. I have chosen to follow Christ, yes; but that doesn't make Christianity my religion. It's God's. It's his initiative, his action, his grace, his revelation, his plan. I'm just thankful he has given me grace to enter into the relationship he has called me to. For that reason, tomorrow on Thanksgiving, as on every other day, I will humbly and heartily thank God for the Cross of Christ, where I was rescued from death.

74

I thank God, too, that the story did not end in death, but in resurrection, glory, and a mission for us to pursue until Christ returns.

Finally: If like me you are thanking God for the Cross, but at the same time you're trying to hold on to the impossible belief that other religions can lead to God, it's time to make your choice.

November 23, 2011

The Cross: Not One of the Universe's Nice Ideas

Too many people want to list all the world's religions on a menu of what I call "nice ideas the universe has for us." By that I mean that there's supposedly a long list of good ways to come to a good ending after we die, and we're free to select any item of that list based on our personal preference.

My purpose in this piece is to show how the Cross of Christ could never go on such a list, and even those who disbelieve in Jesus should be able to see that's so.

Dallas Willard writes in *The Divine Conspiracy* (p. 335),

> "God," Paul said, "makes clear the greatness of his love for us through the fact that Christ died for us while we were still rebelling against him" (Rom. 5:8).
>
> The exclusiveness of the Christian revelation of God lies here. No one can have an adequate view of the heart and purposes of the God of the universe who does not understand that he permitted his Son to die on the cross to reach out to all, even to those who hated him. That is who God is. But that is not just a "right answer" to a theological question. It is God looking at me from the cross with compassion, and providing for me, with never-failing readiness to take my hand to walk on through life.

God's deep, gracious love is proved in the price he paid on our behalf. Christ died for us. He died in love, to bring us to God, to break down the sin barrier between us and God.

One could explain how the cross of Christ accomplished that: how sin had separated us from God, earning us death, and how

Christ paid that price for us. The price that God imposed, God paid. The price was death (Romans 3:23). God made the payment through the death of God the Son, Jesus Christ. He was the One the Father called his beloved, who proclaimed his own eternal unity with the Father (John 10:30, John 17). This beloved one died by crucifixion, among the most torturous methods of execution ever practiced on earth.

But as Willard recalls the love of God that led God to do this for us, he throws in that terrible cultural hand grenade, the word *exclusiveness.* But he had to. It's really quite inescapable. If the Christian message is at all true, then it is exclusively true. It cannot be one of several options. It is either exclusively true or it is thoroughly wrong.

Though this may be difficult, in an age when pluralism and inclusivism are considered among the chief virtues, still I think anyone might be able to see this necessity. It's impossible to include Christianity — the kind of Christianity that centers on the life, death, and resurrection of Christ — in a list of possible ways to know God. Even if one doubts Jesus ever said what he did about being the only way to God (as in John 14:6, for example), it should be clear that he cannot be one of many items on a spiritual menu.

For let us consider what it would mean if he were. Suppose Eckhart Tolle and Oprah and the Bahá'ís and all the other inclusivists are right. Suppose Christianity is one of many paths to God, to enlightenment, fulfillment, Nirvana, or whatever the real goal is.

In that case, the universe offers us many ways to reach our best destiny. But let's follow that thought a bit further. What is that destiny? Different religions have different views, but they agree that it's something. Whatever reality is at its core, there's something about it that gives humans a real place, a real direction, a real destiny. Somehow in some personal or impersonal (and therefore metaphoric) way, therefore, the universe has us in mind, and

77

it offers us all kinds of ways to flourish for now and for beyond. What's our part? We just have to pick one of those ways off the universe's spiritual menu. Let's see, will I have the T-bone or the tofu?

Reality isn't too picky, on this view. It's nice to us, in a way. It gives us freedom to choose. You can follow any number of paths, many of which really are rather nice ideas. Experiencing the "Now" (per Tolle) is a nice idea. New Age spirituality of all kinds fits well into the "nice" category. Rhonda Byrnes *The Secret* tells us everything will go well if we'll just think more positively.

Those are some nice, attractive options aren't they. Let's just make sure we include Jesus. The cross of Christ is, well, another choice among all the nice choices on the spiritual menu. Wasn't that sweet of God the Father to offer his own Son's torture and death as one of our options?

NO!

It doesn't fit, does it? It doesn't belong on any menu of nice ideas! When Jesus looked ahead to the cross it was in agony, his sweat dripping as blood. And that was even before he was arrested. He knew what was coming.

His friends and followers deserted him — as he knew they would do. Was that one of the universe's nice ideas for us?

He was cruelly tortured and mocked. Was that one of the universe's nice ideas for us?

He hung on that infamously cruel cross, dying in excruciating pain while the crowds laughed at him. Was that one of the universe's nice ideas for us?

He was stabbed in the side, so that water and blood flowed out. Was that one of the universe's nice ideas for us?

His body was wrapped up and left in the dark of a rock-hewn tomb. Was that one of the universe's nice ideas for us?

No. There is nothing nice about the cross. It's unthinkable that it would be an item on some spiritual menu, one choice among many, something we could feel free to pass over in favor of warm thoughts, positive thinking, or any other supposed path to God.

Christ's resurrection makes manifest the glory of both his death and his life. It redeems the loss of his death. It makes its greatness even greater. But it does not make it nice. And it hardly supports anyone's view that Christ is just one of many enlightened ones!

C.S. Lewis said in another context, "But let us not come with any patronising nonsense about his being a great human teacher. He has not left that open to us. He did not intend to."

Neither did he leave open the possibility that he might be just one of many spiritual options. *He did not intend to.*

July 16, 2008

The Shrinking Lies of Sin

This is a quick piece, included because it fits so well with the two that follow. I didn't write the three as a series, but they work well that way. Here I open the topic of the series by discussing how sin makes our souls small. In the next piece I speak of God as a soul builder; then in the third I discuss how God calls us to be great. It's all about refusing to be less than God meant us to be.

A popular hymn in the church where I grew up began, "I was sinking deep in sin." I think another song could be written, "I was shrinking deep in sin," for it seems to me that one effect of sin is to make us smaller.

God created us to live large. Genesis 1:28, the first commandment of them all, is simply huge:

> And God blessed them. And God said to them, "Be fruitful and multiply and fill the earth and subdue it and have dominion over the fish of the sea and over the birds of the heavens and over every living thing that moves on the earth."

Jesus stated his purpose in John 10:10: "The thief comes only to steal and kill and destroy. I came that they may have life and have it abundantly."

This is what we were meant for. It is about living life to the full, experiencing the best and the most that life has to offer.

Temptation's Lies

Temptation lies to us and says sin has more to offer. My own experience tells me otherwise. Sin narrows my experience, rather than broadening it. If it is sexual temptation, it constricts my view of the woman. The 1970s feminists were on the right track when they objected to being regarded as sex objects. The woman is a whole person. A purely sexual view regards her in one limited dimension.

It does not make her less of a whole person; it does not shrink her. It shrinks instead the man who falsely sees her as so much less than a whole person. Sexual relations within a faithful, loving marriage are not that way, for the relationship itself is much larger than that, involving a day-long, life-long covenant between two whole people; and marital relationships (unlike most illicit ones, where this is strictly guarded against) have the potential of enlarging into an entire new life in the family.

How Sin Shrinks Us

That is but one example. I could also mention the temptation to anger and impatience at a slow driver blocking the road ahead. What does that anger do but narrow our focus to the bumper in front of us? Nothing exists for us in the whole glorious world but the back end of some annoying car. The sin of impatient anger hides from us that there is a real human in that car. It obscures our view of the rest of the world around us.

It is the same with all sin. Gluttony reduces our world to that of food. Greed reduces our view to what we wish we had. Sloth reduces our world to what we can see and do from our couch. Pride limits our perspective to our own selves.

Sin, which tries to tell us it will enlarge experience, instead makes small our experience of the world. It lies. Above all it shuts out our view of the greatest, largest reality of all, God himself. To seek God and his way is to experience the fullest and best that life has to offer.

February 24, 2010

God Is a Soul Builder

I don't know how to speak this topic well enough. It would take a poet. God's goodness is beyond our comprehension. His goodness is good enough even to overcome suffering, to make beauty out of it, and to build souls for eternity through it. For that is his ultimate purpose in our lives, or at least one way of looking at his purpose.

God is good, and his way is good. It's very good. It's rich, it's beautiful, it's multi-dimensional, it's mysterious where it ought to be, and it's plain where it should be. It's dizzyingly satisfying. It's glorious. It's right.

I don't know how to say that well enough, partly because there's an aspect in it of "you had to be there." You could go there, actually, because what I'm talking about is the long conversation with skeptic Bill L on a blog post titled "The Range Master and the Doctor: A Parable About Abortion."[5] More than anything else, what we talked about in that thread was *suffering* in relation to abortion. Bill L's view is that a fetus cannot suffer before 21 weeks in the womb, so there's no moral harm in taking its life:

> I believe the most reasonable approach we can take with abortion and deciding any right-to-life issue is the point at which something can suffer. By that, I mean not only sensing pain, but having the kind of thoughts that allow any creature to comprehend that pain is something bad, and that it wants to avoid this.

He balances this against other suffering:

---

5   https://www.thinkingchristian.net/posts/2015/08/the-range-master-and-the-doctor-a-parable-about-abortion

I hate to say it, but I'm not surprised that you're not aware of the suffering you want to cause. Unwanted children cause many people suffering. Disabled children cause many people suffering. I suggest you start talking to people who have had abortions and actually listen to them.

But God is good, and his goodness is far better than just wanting us to escape suffering. His goodness is of the sort that wants to build us up in our goodness. He's a soul-tester and a soul-builder, not a comfort-manager.

On one level everyone knows this. Though suffering is not good in itself, still God produces good through it. Suffering amplifies souls. There's a rather cryptic saying of Jesus that comes in here, I think. It's in Matthew 25:29, and I hope I'm not violating the context too badly by using it in this way. Jesus says, "For to everyone who has will more be given, and he will have an abundance. But from the one who has not, even what he has will be taken away."

What we are is amplified in suffering. Those who are growing grow even stronger. Those who are shrinking shrink all the more.

Great Souls

The most beautiful souls I know are those who have stood the test. Years ago I knew Bill McDowell, one of the scholars on the translation team for the New King James Version of the Bible (no relation to Josh or Sean McDowell). He had lost his first wife to breast cancer. Around the time I first met him his second wife was also diagnosed with breast cancer, and she too passed away, slowly and painfully.

I didn't know her well enough to see her heart, but I knew Bill, and I'll never forget what he said at the time of her death: "I am so grateful for the love of God and of this church for me." Sure, he was a world-class scholar, yet what really stood out to me was that he was a man of grace, love, and humility, in ways that were both enlarged and revealed through his suffering.

83

Above all — and he would have been very quick to say this! — he was a man who knew the grace and love of Jesus Christ. Before a soul can grow it must become fully alive. This fullness of life is possible only through Christ, who died for us so that we could live in him forever.

We need Jesus Christ even to get started in soul-building. Suffering can play a part in getting us started on the way of Christ. It shows us — the world is bigger than we are. There are evils we cannot control. Some of them come from within. When we discover this, we have a choice. We can fight for the right to be who we are–a self-centered act right from the start; or we can recognize we need outside help to be rescued, mostly from ourselves.

He rescues us through forgiveness, for one thing. Back to the topic of abortion, I think Christians may be too slow to say that although it's really wrong, God can *really forgive* that wrong. He rescues us through reconciling us to himself. We don't just get a clean slate; we get a new life and a new relationship with him.

An Undreamt-Of World of Goodness
When God accomplishes that rescue for us, he reveals a world of goodness we had never dreamed of. It's goodness like Bill McDowell's; goodness like the fruit of the Spirit of God, highlighted in Galatians 5:22–23: love, joy, peace, patience, kindness, goodness, gentleness, and self-control.

These virtues grow in us best when we face and pass the test of suffering. Some of them would be meaningless without it. To grow in such things is far better than to grow in comfort and ease! Again, everyone knows this on some level. Though everyone would like to live in easy comfort, few of us would love being friends with someone whose life had always been that way. Their souls are small.

Everyone knows this on some level, that is, yet some people would still rather have life their own way. They want to define "goodness" for themselves. To want this is to fail the test at the very beginning; for goodness is God's domain. We can approach it, and we can experience it, on his terms only. To try to define it on our own terms is to put ourselves in the place of God.

Why Settle for Mere Comfort?

God is good. He is good in his way, not in ours; but his way of goodness is our best way of goodness. He's offering us all life in his goodness, for now and forever. Why would anyone settle for mere comfort?

I fear I've been rambling. Don't say I didn't warn you: I told you at the beginning, I don't know how to speak this well enough. My heart is overflowing in such a way I'm finding it hard to connect everything in a strictly logical sequence.

I just want you to understand that true goodness — God's goodness — is more multi-dimensional, more beautiful, though sometimes mysterious, yet in every way better than mere human comfort.

Pursue it. Look to Jesus Christ as your way, truth, and life (from John 14:6) Seek God, and you will find him. And you will know that he is good.

August 28, 2015

We're Called to Be Great

This chapter is intended primarily for people who don't think it's for them: those who will look at the title and say, "that's not my calling, I'm not one of the great ones." There was a time when I let that thinking hold me back from leadership and even from writing. But then I made a very startling discovery in Scripture, and I realized I had a wrong view of Christian humility, and a wrong view of what God calls us to be.

This, along with the article on "The Map and the Fuel," has been probably one of my two most life-changing discoveries in God's word. This first appeared in Discipleship Journal *in December 2008.*

I'm convinced one of the failings of the church in our age is that you and I, "ordinary Christians," have not responded to God's call to be great.

I'm not referring here primarily to the greatness of soul that all of us are to seek: the true depth of worshipful yieldedness to God, and love for him and for our neighbors, that mark the truly mature follower of Christ. Greatness in that sense is crucial to what I am focusing on, but it is not my topic here.

There is another meaning of "greatness," which has to do with how large one's influence is upon one's community and world. It's the greatness of leadership, of impact. This kind of greatness seems to scare us away. Though not all may be called to it, I believe more of us have been called than have responded. We are at risk of missing a great opportunity to change our world and experience the incredible thrill of seeing God do mighty things through us. The world is poorer for it, and we're missing out on the joy we could be living.

The World Needs Great Christians

The world needs to feel the power of true Christian leadership. Some time ago I heard Admiral Richard Denton, USN (Ret.), himself a leader of considerable impact, speaking about his release from prison in Vietnam in 1973 following more than seven-and-a-half years as a prisoner of war. He spoke of how Christ gave him peace and serenity while living in cramped cells and conditions of torture.

I was especially intrigued, though, by his comments on re-entering the world following years of isolation. They showed the returning POWs a newsreel review of U.S. and world events; things he had missed since 1965. His abrupt exposure to the country's moral decline upset him so greatly that after half an hour of viewing, he was sick enough to vomit.

That was more than forty years ago. Who could deny that our world is in worse moral condition now than it was then? Who wouldn't want to see Christ and his Kingdom really change our world — for many to commit their lives to Him, and for his imprint to be pressed anew on the cultural landscape? There are still billions who need to hear the good news of Jesus Christ. This will only happen if men and women of God — ones who are great in their soul — stand up and claim an impact that will be great.

The body of Christ needs both kinds of greatness, greatness of soul and greatness of effect. Greatness of impact certainly includes (among other possible roles) the idea of being a "great leader," one whose influence is felt by thousands. Most of us may not be called to that, but I wonder: Even if we're not called to that level of leadership, *isn't it at least possible that God is calling us to be greater than we are?* Could we be missing opportunities to expand our influence for Christ's glory?

But it's rare to hear a pastor urging us to dare to be great. We have an aversion to the whole idea. I believe there are two major reasons for this. The first is a mistaken understanding about what the Bible teaches regarding greatness and humility.

Humility is certainly among the chief virtues. Jesus said he "did not come to be served, but to serve" (Mark 10:45). Shortly before his crucifixion, his disciples argued over who would be greatest in his kingdom, and Jesus rebuked them for it. In the Beatitudes he tells us it is the meek who will inherit the earth. Many who would be great have stumbled badly over their own pride.

Still, there is greatness throughout the Scriptures, evidenced by godly men and women who were willing to step forward and lead. Consider Moses, Joshua, the great kings of Israel and Judah, Esther, the powerful prophets, the apostles.

John the Baptist: Great in Humility, Humble in Greatness

Consider especially the amazing humility, yet boldness, of John the Baptist, as seen in John 1. Here is humility personified! "I baptize with water," he says, "but there stands One among you whom you do not know. It is he who, coming after me, is preferred before me, whose sandal strap I am not worthy to lose" (John 1:26b, 27). John is the one who clothed himself in goatskins, who ate locusts and wild honey, who eagerly turned over all his followers to Christ when he arrived on the scene, one who gladly said, "He must increase, but I must decrease" (John 3:30).

How then could he say what he said about himself? You may not have noticed it; it's easy to miss. The Jewish leaders had sent messengers to ask him who he was and how he claimed the authority to baptize, that is, to establish a prominent new religious movement outside of their authority. They asked him if he was the Christ, or Elijah, or the Prophet (the one predicted very early by Moses). He denied them all. So they said, "Then who are you?" His answer finally rang out clear: "I am 'The voice of one crying in the wilderness: make straight the way of the Lord,' as the prophet Isaiah said" (John 1:23).

Now, let me paraphrase that to give you a clearer sense of what his listeners heard when he said that. John's answer was in a very definite sense, *"I am — since you asked, and you wouldn't quit asking — one of the three or four most important people in the history of this nation!"* This messenger was one of the most anxiously awaited people in all of prophecy, second only to the Messiah whom he would herald. When John claimed that identity, he took the title of one for whom Israel had been waiting for 700 years! John claimed greatness in high degree.

So then, is this really humility? Absolutely! But it is of a kind we seldom see. The explanation is in a simple statement in verse 6: "There was a man sent from God, whose name was John." John was sent by God; he was simply doing what he was told to do, and he was doing it for the glory of God, whom he constantly lifted up in the person of Jesus Christ.

John was both humble and great at the same time. There are many such examples in the Bible. Isaiah's response when he saw the Lord was, "Woe is me, for I am undone! Because I am a man of unclean lips, and I dwell among a people of unclean lips; for my eyes have seen the King, the Lord of Hosts" (Is. 6:5). Yet when God asked, "Whom shall I send, and who will go for Us?" he said, "Here am I! Send me" (v. 8). He humbly confessed his unworthiness, he accepted his call, and he went on to a career that changed kings and battles and nations.

Called to Be Great

God, who sends some of us to positions of greater prominence and influence, chooses who may have greatness of impact or leadership. Our part is to recognize what God has called us to, to trust in him to accomplish it through us, and to direct all glory to Jesus Christ. Indeed, this is the greatness of spirit that all of us are called to seek.

In some people it will produce more widely visible fruit than others. This is the choice of God, for he gives some of us more opportunity than others. In Matthew 25:14–30, one man received five talents, one received two, and another only one. The ones who received five and two brought a return to their master of five and two respectively. Even though the second one brought back less than half than the first, he received the same commendation: "Well done, good and faithful servant; you were faithful over a few things, I will make you ruler over many things. Enter into the joy of your lord." The exact same words are used in both Matthew 25:21 and 25:23.

So we can see that those who are not asked to enter leadership of widespread impact are no less of value to God than those who are. Still they are expected to be faithful with what they are given. The one who received just one talent brought nothing back with it; he was the one who was censured. His lack of understanding of his master, his lack of faith, and his fear caused him to end with disapproval.

God chooses leaders according to his own will. We see this throughout the Bible, beginning with Abraham, continuing through many others like Moses, David, Esther, Mary, the twelve, and Paul. What these men and women shared in common was the calling of God and their response of humility, faith, and obedience; and also that their lives made a great deal of difference in the world.

Humble, Not Puny
The call is to be humble, not puny. When Jesus rebuked the disciples for jockeying for position in his kingdom, he invited them at the same time to greatness — as long as it was greatness on the right terms: "Whoever desires to become great among you, let him be your servant. And whoever desires to be first among you, let him be your slave" (Matthew 20:26b, 27).

God chooses public greatness (church-wide, community-wide, or even broader in scope) for certain people and not for others. But I fear there are many of us whom God has called in that way, who have not listened, trusted, and obeyed. Some of us could be great for God, legitimately called by him; but we've turned our back on it. This is a great loss to the kingdom of God. It is the burying of the talents, for which God offers only rebuke. To dare to be great, as we follow what God has called us to, is to be humble and obedient.

Ready to Pay the Price

There is more to learn about greatness from John the Baptist, this time from the account in Luke. It uncovers the second chief reason we approach the topic of greatness with fear:

> Then he said to the multitudes that came out to be baptized by him, "Brood of vipers! Who warned you to flee from the wrath to come? Therefore bear fruits worthy of repentance, and do not begin to say to yourselves, "We have Abraham as our father." For I tell you that God is able to raise up children of Abraham from these stones. And even now the ax is laid to the root of the trees.

> Therefore every tree which does not bear good fruit is cut down and thrown into the fire." So the people asked him, saying, "What shall we do then?" He answered and said to them, "He who has two tunics, let him give to him who has none; and he who has food, let him do likewise." Then tax collectors also came to be baptized, and said to him, "Teacher, what shall we do?" And he said to them, "Collect no more than what is appointed for you." Likewise the soldiers asked him, saying, "And what shall we do?" So he said to them, "Do not intimidate anyone or accuse falsely, and be content with your wages."

> And with many other exhortations he preached to the people. But Herod the tetrarch, being rebuked by John concerning Herodias, his brother Philip's wife and for all the evils which

Herod had done, also added this, above all, that he shut John up in prison (Luke 3: 7–14, 18–20 NKJV).

John stirred things up a great deal. *He paid a price for it in the end.* (Jesus himself did the same, even more so.) John knew what he was called to do; it included agitating for change in a corrupt culture. Some responded gladly. The king, however, threw him in prison, and later had him executed. Greatness pays a price. Even "successful" greatness — such as the greatness of Daniel, of Joseph, of many others in our day who are seeing great fruit in churches, mission agencies, government, and military — pays a price of long hours, much opposition, deep concerns, many pains.

Trusting in God

I think I have too often refused to step toward greatness because of fear: fear of stirring people up, fear of being branded, fear of having to give up the easy way. The cost of this has been a loss of the thrilling opportunity to see what God could do through me if I followed him wherever he led. The further cost is that the glory of God, which I could have conveyed to many in the wider world, has been hidden like a light under a bushel.

John the Baptist's desert example is a hard one to follow. God does not call many of us to make a solitary stand for him in that way. He does call each of us individually to decide we will follow him wherever he leads; that is a decision we can only make for ourselves. From there, though, most of us will find opportunities to follow God into greatness by doing it with teams of brothers and sisters in Christ.

Oh, for communities of faith determined to change their cities and their world! Oh, to belong to a band of believers who will charge the enemy's ground and take it back for Jesus Christ!

Discovering Our Sphere of Impact

How then can we know whether we're called to be great in this sense? It's not that difficult.

First, we need to recall the other kind of greatness that we alluded to at the beginning, the greatness that founded in a deep relationship with God. It starts in knowing his will as revealed in Scripture, seeking his face and his guidance daily, and knowing the power of the Holy Spirit in our lives. It certainly includes knowing what true humility is all about.

Second, each of us has a sphere of influence, whether narrow or broad. That's where we begin, by seeking to have maximum impact where we already can. We have our talents in hand from the master, and we can see what return we can bring him from them.

Third, we can explore the edges of that circle to see how our influence can expand. We can risk going out on a limb, influencing a wider group of people, studying and learning to expand our capabilities, trying new things to multiply our impact.

Christ taught that the one who is faithful in a little will be entrusted with much. Starting where we are and walking by faith, there's no telling how much God will lead us to do for him.

It's wise to seek depth before breadth: to do one thing well before attempting many, to influence one person deeply before trying to lead a crowd. Doing "one thing well" — or many things, for that matter — involves knowing how God has gifted us and putting our focus in those areas. Our gifts are a great clue to our calling.

Fourth, we can profit from the encouragement of a community of brothers and sisters who are committed to the same things. It's hard to go it alone. Together, though, we can burn brightly for God. Going for greatness often means hard word and risks, both of which are much easier when someone is standing at your side to encourage.

It may be that the first step into the edge of your circle would be to gather a group like this. It's not just a Bible study, not just an accountability group; it's an action/encouragement group.

Can we revive a true understanding of greatness? In seeking God's glory alone, can we pursue it in the widest, deepest, most influential, most thrilling way? What could hold us back, if we would just seek to know and to go and do what God has sent us to do?

Let's put aside weakness masquerading as humility. Let's lay aside fear, and take up faith and courage instead. Let's choose to be as great as God has called us to be, so his glory may shine brightly and widely.

November 23, 2015

Part 2: Thinking Christianly

While this whole book is an exercise in thinking Christianly, I'm narrowing it down to a closer focus in part 2: What does it mean to be a thinking Christian, and to be in a thinking fellowship?

Thinking Christianly: Ten Essentials

What does it take to think Christianly? This is just a list, on one view of it. But it's a list to ponder, perhaps even to view as a checklist for your own Christian thinking. Why does it matter? That's pretty much the point of the whole book.

My blog's title, *Thinking Christian* isn't so much about how I view myself but about what I hope to encourage: thinking Christianly: thinking well, thinking deeply, thinking in accordance with the truth of God revealed through Jesus Christ.

But what does it mean to think Christianly? Here are ten quick answers. Thinking Christianly means...

1. *Recognizing that the truth of God in Jesus Christ is always our reference point.* Charles Colson rightly said the answer to the question, "What is Christianity?" is that it is the explanation for everything." Of course, he did not mean that everything is explained in the Bible, but that the Bible reveals the framework of truth overarching all of reality. To think otherwise is to think other than Christianly.

2. *Being a disciple of Jesus Christ.* The word "disciple" means "follower-learner." It's no accident that one of Jesus' primary activities on earth was teaching.

3. *Submitting oneself to the discipline of study* (1 Timothy 3:15). It's not always easy; easy discipleship was never promised us.

4. *Developing in the knowledge of God* — through Scripture primarily, but also through human teachers, whether live, through other listening, or through reading; and through reflection on personal experience.

5. *Developing extra-biblical knowledge.* If we can learn from the ants (Proverbs 6:6–11), then obviously the world has much to

teach us! The men of Issachar were commended for under-standing their times (1 Chronicles 12:32). Paul quoted two Greek poets in Acts 17 and Titus 1:12. Thinking Christianly is not just knowing and thinking about the Bible. It is much wider in its application than that.

6. *Honoring questions.* It's about letting the questions work in us; letting them bother us; being willing to let questions re-main questions until answered, and knowing which ones to chase to the ground until we have the answer. Nothing is more disastrous to Christian thinking than, "We shouldn't ask that question."

7. *Learning how to think well.* This means understanding how to think widely, by gaining a breadth of knowledge; to think deeply by spending reflective time on some limited, focused areas of importance; and to think accurately by developing mental tools for excellence in thinking, especially logic.

8. *Learning to connect biblical principles to other spheres of life,* such as work, law, education, politics, arts, media, and so on.

9. *Starting from where you are,* whatever your background, edu-cation, or aptitudes may be, and...

10. *Taking the next steps of growth from there.*

January 25, 2010

Apologetics and Apologists: Purpose and Motivation

Thinking Christianly has a lot to do with understanding Christian apologetics, or reasons to believe in Christ. Sometimes, though, it has too much to do with apologetics. That is, the field of apologetics is prone to taking an inward turn that belies what it means to think Christianly. We have to first see, then understand, then resist that temptation.

Some are describing our day as a "Golden Age" of apologetics. I agree; the evidence is everywhere. Academic research is booming. Conferences are sprouting up everywhere. Books are selling.

More to the point, we have great answers to hard questions like never before, and new research keeps bringing us more. So this is a great time to be in apologetics, to be the person with answers.

It's also a time that's rife with risk, the risk of doing the right thing for the wrong reason. It can derail your relationship with Christ if you're not careful.

The Motivated Core Group

Having answers is great. It feels good. What feels even better is being affirmed for having answers.

That affirmation comes from two opposite places. First, there are those who agree and support your answers, which means other people who are deeply interested in questions and answers: others involved with apologetics, that is. Where it *really* gets motivational is when others link to your blog page, publish your articles or books, or invite you to speak.

But this is all about people who agree already, isn't it? It can become ingrown; a self-reinforcing closed circle of people encouraging one another in their mutual interest in apologetics.

The Loyal (?) Opposition

But it's not as if the circle is entirely closed, for there is another set of people who are deeply interested in Christian apologetics: skeptics, atheists, and others who disagree. These are the P. Z. Myerses, the John Loftuses, the Richard Dawkinses, the Sam Harrises (why do all their last names end with *s*?) and all the social media commenters who think our answers are all wrong. They keep us questioning, and they keep us challenged. If there's anything lacking in our answers, we'll find out about it seen enough from them.

For those of us who enjoy a little fight over our answers, this too is highly motivational.

But even though this side circle of skeptics is pretty substantial, it's still a relatively closed group.

The Inward Turn

Which is where the danger lies. All this can easily turn into a production factory churning out psychological strokes to motivate people with an apologetics bent. And speaking of "bent," the motivational effect is to bend me (and others like me) inward toward the closed circle of like-minded (or totally opposite-minded) people.

The effect is multiplied in the case of blogs. Most bloggers write what interests them. When I'm blogging, the circle of interest doesn't have to be any larger than one person: me.

I'm painting with broad strokes, obviously. I could name lots of exceptions: leaders and others who are resisting that inward turn. At the risk of leaving many more than I'm including, I could mention Josh McDowell, Mark Mittelberg, Lee Strobel, Frank

Turek, Greg Koukl, and the whole Ratio Christi movement, among many others who are people bucking this tide.

And I don't want this to come across as if it were some deep secret I've uncovered, hiding in some dark corner of the apologetics world somewhere. Here's how I found out about it: I observed it in myself. It's nothing more or less than what comes with being human. Yet God does not want us to be content living on a merely human plane of operation (1 Cor. 3:3).

Purpose
The effect is strong. It's hard to break free of. I really do like the links from other blogs, the high rankings I've received from Feedspot and the other publishing and speaking opportunities I get. I'm sure I'm not the only one like that. If we're doing it all for the closed circle, though, we're wasting our time. There are millions of people outside the circle who need encouragement with their questions.

To Serve
Jesus Christ didn't come to teach us how to get strokes, after all. Speaking of himself, he said, "For even the Son of Man did not come to be served but to serve, and to give his life as a ransom for many" (Mark 10:45).

And If I might be permitted to borrow a line of thought Jesus used in a different concept (Luke 5:31), those who are already equipped have no need of an equipper — even though in this case they are the ones most likely to support and encourage the equipping. So apologetics needs to break free of that circle. As I've already said, this is happening among some. It needs to happen more. I myself need to break free.

To Encourage
And there are others outside the circle who really do want the equipping. They just don't always know how to ask for it. I think the big issue is that we apologists have been so caught among our

own group, we've lost track of how to connect with others outside of it. Ask an average church member if they're interested in apologetics, and their most likely answer will be, "Huh?" They don't even know the term. But ask the same church member if they want their children to be solid and confident in the faith, or if they've ever been puzzled by hard questions, and you're very likely to hear them say "Yes, absolutely!" It's the same question either way, except it's spoken in different language.

Breaking Free

Blogging and apologetics are both prone to inward-focused motivational patterns. We've got to keep our spiritual guard up against that. Christians are called not to be served, not to be stroked, but to serve, and to give our lives in service for many.

April 6, 2013

9 Practical Ways to Build Discipleship of the Mind in Your Local Church

So then, what if you're hoping to grow Christian thinking in your local fellowship? How can you do it without leaving behind some people who are less oriented toward deep thinking? This set of suggested answers is mostly for pastors and other teachers.

Like my earlier "Ten Essentials" article in this section of the book, it's just a short list, but don't let that fool you: It could be powerful in your church.

Here are some short seed thoughts for pastors who want to raise the level of discussion and build discipleship of the mind in your church, without leaving any listeners behind. It's only a beginning; I'm sure the entire list of possible ways could number 900 or 9000.

1. Ask during sermon prep, "Who might have a problem with this message I'm preaching? What might they consider hard about it — hard to believe, hard to accept, hard to live?" State that problem in your sermon, *then give a good answer!* Timothy Keller's sermons are masterful examples. Recognize that he's adapted his message to his Manhattan congregation; you'll want to adjust yours to your own. You needn't quote every author he quotes. Wherever you are, though, you can still ask the problem question and give an answer.

2. Include a "For further thought" question list in the bulletin. Make the questions meaty. Encourage Sunday school classes to work through the questions. Even an after-church restaurant group could grab one of the questions for part of their conversation.

3. Teach something everyone can understand but few already know. Show a map of Jesus' walking travels. Tell something about how fishermen worked in the Sea of Galilee. Explain why Paul felt such a need to take a strong tone with the Galatians and the Corinthians.

4. Use Lydia McGrew's *Hidden in Plain View* to spice up your teaching. You'll be blown away when you discover how amazingly interesting it is, how new it is to almost everyone — and how easy it is to teach.

5. Teach paradoxes. For example: How could John the Baptist be such an incredible model of humility, and yet still tell people he was the fulfillment of the great Isaiah 40 prophecy? *Was that humble, too?* (I'll never forget the lesson I learned when I asked that question: It's in this book as "Called to Be Great.")

6. Consider teaching more challenging sermons once in a while. You know you can't meet everyone's needs in a sermon, so perhaps you've been meeting the needs of those who want a less challenging message all this time. But maybe two to three times a year you can devote a Sunday to aiming higher.

7. Prepare two sermons. If a church can have a traditional and a contemporary service, why can't it have an introductory sermon and a more advanced one, in two different services?

8. Think outside the sermon box — and outside yourself, too. Open up other opportunities, elsewhere in your church's calendar and teaching schedule, for other teachers to go deeper. But don't leave them out in the cold! Support their ministry. Talk those teachings up during your sermon once in a while.

9. Take the big risk! (In the following essay I say this has "the potential to get a pastor fired for following Jesus' example.") Do what Jesus did, and leave some big questions unanswered at the end of your sermon. Then (as Jesus also did, see Matthew 13), offer a follow-up session for the really interested disciples to come find out more.

I'm sure you've noticed these are all directed toward pastors. Lay person, if you think your pastor needs to hear this, he very well might. Feel free to share it — but do it with love and patience, as someone who's on his side, remembering that he's got his hands full already. (Pastor, if someone comes blasting you with this, let me know. I'll post their names publicly on a blog wall of shame on my blog!)

September 7, 2017

Five Reasons Churches Need More Unanswered Questions

I believe churches today get some of their message and their method seriously wrong, even if their beliefs are right and true. The problem that remains is that we answer too many questions too quickly. That wasn't Jesus' way. But could we ever change direction and do it as he did?

I must begin with a caution: This has the potential to get pastors fired for following Jesus' example.

It will also confuse anyone who sees me as a Christian apologist, and apologetics as being in the business of giving answers. But the fact is I believe we need more unanswered questions. Pastors, in particular, need to leave more questions unanswered.

While I'm sure that sounds revolutionary, I can't help but come to that conclusion. Jesus set the example, as best seen in the book of John. There are (at least) five reasons.

1. To Follow Jesus' Example

Jesus asked question after question after question. They weren't always easy. His first words in the gospel of John are a question: "What are you seeking?" His introductory statement to Nathaniel provokes sheer confusion. When his mother asks him to help with the wine in Cana, he responds to her with a question that reader of the gospel have struggled to understand ever since. In Jerusalem he bewilders the Jews by telling them he will raise up "this temple" in three days. Nicodemus offers him the honor of recognizing he came from God, and Jesus says, "You must be born again." What?

Need more? He puzzles the woman at the well with an offer of living water. He asks Philip (a native of that region) where they can buy bread to feed thousands (again, what?). He drives the multitude away with truly incomprehensible teachings about eating his flesh and drinking his blood, and then he asks his close followers, "Will you leave, too?" He confuses the Jews by telling them where he is going, they cannot come.

And so it continues. I could point to similar tactics of our Lord in the Synoptic gospels. His Beatitudes open up at least as many questions open as they answer. He explains his parables only to a few (Matthew 13). When the Jews ask him where he gets his authority, he asks them whether John's baptism is from heaven or from men.

2. To Prepare Ears to Hear

Of course, I do not mean to say that Jesus never answered anyone's questions, or never followed through so as to satisfy hearers concerning the questions he raised. It was always a matter of timing and of sensitivity to the Spirit and his audience.

The unifying principle is this: He gave answers to those who were ready to hear. ("Let him who has ears to hear....") The rest he goaded toward readiness with unanswered questions that stimulate their curiosity and provoked dissatisfaction with where they were. He staunchly refused to inoculate them with half-received truths.

Even the Sermon on the Mount, for all its simple clarity, must have provoked considerable consternation when he gave it. It certainly does that for me. I don't know about you, but there are places in it where I have trouble understanding just what he meant, and I have to dig in hard to figure it out; and there are even more places where I have more trouble yet understanding how I can live up to it. It is not a sermon meant to satisfy on the surface.

3. To Accomplish Your Real Purpose

Of course, Jesus' model is a problematical one to follow. I can't remember the last Sunday sermon I heard that left me wondering "what?" the way Jesus' messages so often did. I don't know how any pastor could keep his job doing what Jesus did. It's the pastor's job to provide answers, isn't it?

No, actually, it's the pastor's job to lead the flock toward richness of life and service in Christ.

Often this means turning us, as listeners, away from habits or beliefs that lead toward death. The difficulty with that is that it means leading us to change, which few of us will do as long as our current ways seem to be working for us. But let me state it baldly, okay? We don't change very much without pain.

Answers soothe. They hardly ever produce the pain that leads to change. Unanswered questions rankle, however. They throw us off balance. The right questions might just jostle us out of our conditions of comfort so that we can see what's not really working for us after all.

Some questions can help us see the distance between who we think we are (Nicodemus, the teacher of Israel, for example) and who we really are (spiritually ignorant and confused, in his case).

4. To Do the Questions Justice

Then a further reason to leave some questions open is because even a sermon-length answer may be too short to do them justice. Some questions are really hard. To compress their answers into thirty minutes — intro and illustrations included — may well be misleading; and the more serious thinkers in the congregation will know it. Some of them may even start to wonder whether all of Christianity is equally superficial. This applies equally to questions of intellect and of application, by the way.

5. To Answer the Questions They're Really Asking

I am of course an apologist, one whose business it is to understand and to communicate answers. I could dream (if I dared!) of the day when my wisdom was so manifest that every answer I gave was unquestioned. Alas, it is a dream: it didn't happen even to Jesus!

There is another sort of unquestioned answer, though, that happens in thousands of churches every Sunday: it is the answer given by preachers to un-questions. Teachers explain how to be more like Christ when they don't even know if their congregations are asking that question. Pastors teach how to show God's Kingdom love in their communities, when there's little sign that anyone is wondering about that. And the people walk away with answers, never having felt any urgency to know, or any deep need to practice.   SIN

So how do we get the people asking the right questions? By making them questions, not just answers. Once they finally do get around to asking the right questions, they'll be on the edge of their seats waiting for an answer!

When to Answer After All

A leader's questions can also encourage followers to ask questions, in other words which is often the very best thing for us. How can we understand better, after all, unless we probe deeper?

Which leads to the point at which the pastor/teacher really must be prepared to supply answers: when the people are finally asking — when they desperately need to know.

Too often this happens only when life causes pain. "Why, God?" is the most frequently articulated question of them all, followed by, "How will I make it through this?" These are great questions; the Psalms are replete with them. But they are not the only ones, and not always the most important. They do tend quite reliably to be expressed when they need to be.

Not all questions are so reliably brought into the open. Many of them we should be asking but often aren't. "How can I truly be more like Christ?" "What would God have us do to show his

Kingdom love in this community?" Or, "How do I know it's even true?"

More Unanswered Questions

I suspect — I hope! — this has raised a lot of questions for you. One of them, I'm sure, is how it would be received if you shifted to following Jesus' pattern by leaving more questions unanswered.

But of course I must close with a question of my own: Can you imagine what it would be like to teach your answers to a congregation that had learned the value of questions — that had questions of their own — and was ready and eager to hear the answers? Then I suggest you emphasize questions, just as Jesus did.

May 14, 2013

The Crucial Need for Intellectual Engagement

As a supported missionary with Cru for many years, then Ratio Christi, and now (as part of my vocation today) with Global Service Network, I have <u>ministry partners</u> who support my work financially. One of them wrote an email asking me to clarify something I'd said about the need for Christians to grow in our mental awareness and engagement. It was a good question, and I've decided to share my answer more broadly here.

Thank you for your thoughtful email. It's good to hear from you. I appreciate your comments about prayer and service — which are certainly high priority in the Christian life.

Regarding mental awareness and engagement, I would first of all place that in the context of knowing God and His word, which comes first always. The words "know" and "knowledge" appear at least 377 times in the New Testament, depending on which translation you use. In my Bible, that averages out to more than two occurrences per page. Add to that the 123 or more occurrences of different forms of "teach" and you reach something like 600 related occurrences.

Other key words are used surprisingly less often. "Faith" appears 227 times, "believe" is used 105 times, and "love" 172 times, according to the software I'm using.

Romans 12:1–2 are crucial: We are transformed by the renewing of our minds. The fact that God has revealed Himself primarily through a *book* in this age is significant. So knowledge is obviously important.

The Missiological Model

I am quite sure what I've said so far is very close to your heart, that you are deeply committed to it. Knowledge is good in itself; to learn and to understand truth is to become more like Christ.

Sure, there's a warning that "Knowledge puffs up." If it meant that absolutely, though, there could hardly be such a constant emphasis on it throughout Scripture. Any good gift or skill can become a source of pride. That's what we need to watch out for.

What about engaging with the world on these matters, though? On this I prefer to think in missiological terms. A missionary to an African tribe or a city in China has three initial tasks: First, to know and follow Christ increasingly every day; second, to know the language of the people to whom he is ministering; and third, to understand the culture where he is ministering. Then comes the essential job of translating his knowledge of God and His word into terms the people there can understand.

The people the missionary is reaching to in turn need to *learn* the Word of God, and at the same time to *unlearn* their false and idolatrous practices. The missionary must understand the common falsehoods of the culture well enough to show how they fail the test of truth.

For Example:

That's the basic mindset underlying what I have said about being mentally prepared. Now I'll illustrate with an example. Suppose I present Jesus Christ as the truth who sets us free, and do not explore terminology with my audience. In today's culture we will likely stumble badly over that word "truth." I know *what I mean* when I use it, but they don't typically hear it that way.

I've had an actual encounter on the web with a man named Jacob who was convinced there is no such thing as actual truth, that it's all "socially constructed" and therefore contingent on your culture. So I asked, "what about 2+2=4? Would you say that's socially constructed? Could 2+2=5?" He answered, and I quote,

> It is not *necessary* to use the terms "right" and "wrong" — we participate in a culture in which those are familiar resources that we draw on to describe the world in significant ways. Is it necessary to describe the world in any one way in particular? I don't think so. Why? Because the world I live in is not a functionalist system — I am not a cog in a machine.

> The teacher trains the child to emit the signs that the teacher was taught to emit and their teacher was taught to emit and the people that certify teachers were taught to emit. Or said differently, of course $2 + 2 = 5$ is an illegitimate answer. The child will probably be corrected, or retrained, if they said that it was equal to 5.

> What is a "correct understanding"? What do you mean by that turn of phrase? My guess is that a "correct understanding" is one that you happen to agree with or think that others should agree with.

Now, I agree that no amount of arguing will persuade a person like Jacob to change his mind, apart from the powerful work of the Holy Spirit.

"Puffs Up" Isn't the Whole Story

Still I don't think Paul's model for ministry was entirely expressed in that 1 Corinthians passage on "knowledge puffs up." We also have:

- Acts 17:1–3, including, "And he reasoned in the synagogue every Sabbath, and tried to persuade Jews and Greeks."

- Acts 19:8–10: "*And he entered the synagogue and for three months spoke boldly, reasoning and persuading them about the kingdom of God. But when some became stubborn and continued in unbelief, speaking evil of the Way before the congregation, he withdrew from them and took the disciples with him, reasoning daily in the hall of Tyrannus. This continued for two years, so that all the residents of Asia heard the word of the Lord, both Jews and Greeks."*

- 2 Corinthians 5:11: *"Therefore, knowing the fear of the Lord, we persuade others."*

- 2 Corinthians 10:3–5: *"For though we walk in the flesh, we are not waging war according to the flesh. For the weapons of our warfare are not of the flesh but have divine power to destroy strongholds. We destroy arguments and every lofty opinion raised against the knowledge of God, and take every thought captive to obey Christ."*

- Also from 1 Peter 3:15–16: *"But in your hearts regard Christ the Lord as holy, always being prepared to make a defense to anyone who asks you for a reason for the hope that is in you; yet do it with gentleness and respect, having a good conscience, so that, when you are slandered, those who revile your good behavior in Christ may be put to shame."*

- And finally, Jude, verse 3: *"Beloved, although I was very eager to write to you about our common salvation, I found it necessary to write appealing to you to contend for the faith that was once for all delivered to the saints."* (Based on the context, I believe this involves confronting false teaching.)

The 2 Corinthians 10 passage is especially important, because it speaks of a *spiritual warfare* that includes destroying arguments and every lofty opinion raised against the knowledge of God. This aspect of ministry is not *opposed* to spiritual ministry, it is an *essential part* of it. We might also note the many, many times in Acts and in the Epistles that the early Christians appealed to evidences in presenting their case. 1 Corinthians 15:3–6 is one classic example.

Spiritual Formation

This is not only about influencing non-believers, by the way, but also about Christian spiritual formation. More than one study has shown that among young people who are raised in strong churches and yet move away from the faith in early adulthood, the most commonly cited reason has been that they just didn't think it was true. They're confronted with many different truth claims, and they don't have the information or training to recognize there are good reasons to believe Christianity is true. Typically (very typically) they imbibe the modern message that we're all free to choose (or create) our own truth, that whatever truth you decide is true is true because you decide that it is.

In contrast, I have heard from several blog readers that they have been significantly encouraged to learn that atheism/secularism has viable Christian answers, and that this has strengthened their faith considerably.

Thus I conclude, based on the example and instruction of the apostles, and our responsibilities as missionaries and disciplers wherever we live, that Christians are called to understand the is- sues of the day in light of the truth of God's word, and to engage the culture in those issues so as to be able to explain the truth both *clearly* and *persuasively*.

February 25, 2009

Part 3: Positive Apologetics

Apologists often divide their discipline into "positive" and "negative" apologetics. The former is about reasons to believe in Christ, the latter is about reasons not to think skeptics' challenges are damaging to belief. Parts 3, 4 and 5 of this book are all on apologetics, beginning with three new positive arguments for your consideration.

The Two Most Overlooked Apologetics Verses in the Bible

There are different schools of apologetics. One says that the Bible confirms its own truth. Another says we need evidence to support its truth. The good news is we really have evidence supporting it, and as this article shows (and "Too Good to Be False" does, too), sometimes that evidence is right there in the pages of the Bible itself.

This is one of my more philosophically technical articles, but I don't think you need to be a specialist to get real value from its main points.

There's a powerful message hiding inside two very familiar verses in the Old Testament. That message is, *These ancient Hebrews did some advanced thinking, centuries ahead of their time. Either that or they had help: God's revelation.*

The first verse is *really* familiar:

Genesis 1:1 *"In the beginning God created the heavens and the earth."*

The second one comes close:

Exodus 3:13–14a *"Then Moses said to God, If I come to the people of Israel and say to them, ˜The God of your fathers has sent me to you, and they ask me, 'What is his name? — what shall I say to them?' God said to Moses,"* I AM WHO I AM."

The Little-Known Uniqueness of Genesis 1:1
Now, where is there a message hiding in Genesis 1:1? You wouldn't see it just looking at it; you have to compare it with

other religions' and other peoples' creation stores. The account in Genesis is *strikingly* different.

Paraphrasing, then quoting from page 32 and following of *Creation out of Nothing: A Biblical, Philosophical, and Scientific Exploration* by Paul Copan and William Lane Craig:

Genesis is quite unlike other Mesopotamian accounts of the origin of the cosmos. The others are intertwined with accounts of the origins of the gods, their ancestry, and so on. They don't identify these gods as creators. The deity may control some element of the universe, or may "be" that thing. But it's not the creator.

There's nothing like that in Genesis! Quoting from the same source:

> Further, Yahweh simply speaks, thereby creating; in other ANE cosmogonies, deities struggle to divide the waters. Also in Genesis 1, the astral bodies are not gods (as in ANE accounts) but are *creations*....

There's no hint of a struggle in Genesis 1. Continuing:

> Gerhard von Rad makes the powerful point that Israel's worldview, as reflected in Genesis, drew a sharp demarcating line between God and the world. The material world is purged of any quality of the divine or the demonic....

> This is unlike all other creation myths. Genesis is significant simply for its utter uniqueness. There's something there that begs for explanation: What led them to such an utterly unique view of reality?

There is even more to be said, but it will fit better once we've looked at our second "overlooked apologetics verse."

The Advanced Thinking of "I AM WHO I AM"

Moses asked God for his name, his identity. God answered, "I AM WHO I AM."

Consider how unique this is. We know humans through our relationships.

- We're known by our families. "Who is your father?" was the question in the ancient Near East. Today we're still identified through our family names and our family heritage.

- We're identified by our relationship to maleness and femaleness.

- As we grow and develop, our personalities are formed in relation to our relatives, our friends, even our foes or (if your school experience was like many) tormentors.

- Our identity is tied to the land, which is also a relational matter. ("Where are you from? What nationality are you?")

- Our identity is further tied to our work. ("What do you do for a living?")

Now, how are gods known in myth? In exactly the same way: by relationship to one another and to the created order, and by what they do. Their identities too are relational. And so it is with identity in every case. It is *always* relational.

This is what makes Yahweh's answer in Exodus so remarkable. In biblical culture much more than today's, a person's name and identity were wrapped up together with each other. God was known to the Hebrews by many titles, most of which had to do with his role or way of relating to creation: The Almighty, the Lord of Hosts (Armies), The Provider, and so on. He is a relational God, after all.

But in Exodus Moses was apparently asking for something more: God's actual name, which would reveal his full identity, his full relatedness. When God consented to answer, to what relationship did he point? "I AM WHO I AM." He pointed to himself. No other relationship could be adequate to identify him. He was (and is) just who he was (and is).

Advanced Thinking

This is more remarkable than it might seem at first sight. For apologetical purposes we cannot assume that monotheism is true; that would be begging the question most illegitimately. But we can examine its implications: what if it is true?

This kind of examination has been done for centuries. One of its most solid conclusions is that God is "self-existent." He is what he is, without reference to any other being whatever. He is *being itself,* as the philosophers and theologians put it. God is he who "is," to whom the verb "to be" applies uniquely. It literally couldn't be said any better than, "I AM WHO I AM."

I won't go into the advanced philosophical discussion on this. Instead I'll simply point out that a Bronze Age sheepherder's name for God is as accurate a name as could possibly be advanced for a monotheistic God. It's perfect. It couldn't be improved.

God's name, his revealed identity, I AM WHO I AM, has never failed from within the context of monotheistic thought. It has stood many centuries' test of philosophical and theological coherence.

How'd They Do That?

This ties back to Genesis 1:1: God created the heavens and the earth from nothing. Besides himself, nothing was. There was God as pure Being, the totality of all reality. Creation had to be *ex nihilo* — from nothing (no preexisting matter, no material cause) — if there was to be any creation at all. (See my chapter, "Do You Think About God As He Truly Is?" for more on that.)

In other words, these two verses fit perfectly. I don't mean they fit nicely. I mean *perfectly.*

So what's the apologetic point, then?

1. The idea of monotheism, whether it's a *true* idea or not, entails certain metaphysical and theological implications.

2. Centuries of refinement of thought have brought us to a point where it's fair to say that the art of thinking on monotheism has reached an advanced stage — again, whether monotheism is true or not.

3. These centuries of work have never contradicted, but only confirmed, the insights of the author of Genesis and Exodus regarding the nature of God, if there is a God.

4. Genesis and Exodus are completely unique in their statements on these matters.

So Moses, the author of these books, came up with ideas of God that no one ever matched in his day, and no one has improved upon in the centuries since then.

I'd say he did pretty well for a Bronze Age farmer. Either that, or as I said at the top of this essay, he had help. I think the "help" answer is the more likely one by far.

January 23, 2010

A Divine Hiddenness Argument for Christianity

The previous essay was "one of my more technical," I said in introducing it. This one is the most technical of them all. It's an experimental exploration into a new philosophically-oriented argument for the truth of Christianity. And it's for people who want to dig in deep. The essay following this one calms that down considerably again, if you prefer to jump there.

This essay is meant as a conversation-starter, an exploration, not a final word. It starts with what's often considered an argument *against* Christianity based on God's "hiddenness." J. L. Schellenberg proposed a form of this argument, in which he concluded that if God is real and wants people to believe in him, there would be no unbelievers except those who aren't sincerely seeking. If there are sincerely seeking unbelievers, then they should always find God in every case.

The answer to that depends on what it means to be sincerely seeking, and on questions revolving around the sovereignty of God in salvation. I'm not going to address that any further here. I only mention it because that argument and mine share the name "Divine Hiddenness." Otherwise they have little to do with each other. I thought I should make the distinction clear.

I must lay some background as I begin.

Background to the Argument

There's an interesting variant on this divine hiddenness argument against Christianity. An atheist blogger who goes by "Ebon Musings" wrote (paraphrased here),

- There is no visible work of God in the form of miracles in the world today.

124

- Events formerly considered miraculous are now more reasonably treated as myth, fable, or misinterpreted acts of nature.

- Believers claim that God can nonetheless be known and perceived through some faith sense. Quite likely however, this faith sense does not actually exist, due to the unanswerability of questions like, What is it? Where is it? How is it validated or verified, especially in view of contrary reports by different people?

- So even if God exists, if there is no verifiable way of detecting his presence and activity, he may as well not exist.

- God, if he exists, can and should want to reveal himself in some unambiguous way.

In his own words, he writes,

> I would certainly begin to believe in God if I were to witness an unambiguous manifestation of the divine, and the vast majority of atheists probably would as well…What further harm could it possibly do for him to appear and attempt to convince them otherwise?[6]

Because God has not done this, Ebon Musings concludes there is probably no God. This is (in compressed form) his version of the *divine hiddenness argument against Christianity.*

Is God So Hidden?

Now, one glaring weakness in this argument is the billions of people who believe God's existence is well evidenced through apologetic reasoning. And most of those billions, myself included, affirm the "faith sense" of which Ebon Musings spoke, and we deny that it is as hard to define as he says it is. It is the touch of God himself upon his people. If it is hard to explain to others, it is difficult in about the same way it would be to explain "red" to someone blind from birth.

---

6   http://www.ebonmusings.org/atheism/burningbush.html

Additionally, God is evident to us in the beauty and design of nature, in his revelation through Scripture, in the extra-biblical historical support that revelation receives, and in a host of philosophical arguments. The situation, then, is this: we have one group saying that if God existed, he would have made himself more evident than he has, and another group saying he has made himself perfectly evident.

What Kind of Evidence Would Suffice?

The first group is looking, perhaps, for what Ebon Musings called "an unambiguous manifestation of the divine." It's not clear to me what that might be, though I have heard people speak of God appearing like Santa in the Macy's parade,[7] or writing his name in the sky without an airplane. But Peter Boghossian, Lawrence Krauss, and Richard Dawkins, leading atheists all, have said that they'd doubt even that. It could be a mass delusion or something.

So for them, God's signature would have to be completely unmistakable and undeniable. If the so-called non-coding portions of DNA were found to be codes after all — specifically, codes that spelled out the text of the gospel of John — maybe that would do it for them. Then there would be no longer any room for doubt.

I don't think I'm overstating the standard of evidence some skeptics want of God. The fine-tuning of the universe points clearly to a fine-tuner,[8] but those who don't want a God can nevertheless find a way out of that conclusion: an untested, untestable, massively theoretical, Occam's-razor-violating "multiverse."[9] They will gladly violate basic scientific principles to find a "scientific" alternative to God.

---

[7] https://www.thinkingchristian.net/2008/11/the-internal-experience-of-the-holy-spirit/#comment-10297

[8] http://www.godandscience.org/apologetics/designun.html

[9] https://www.thinkingchristian.net/posts/2011/02/if-you-dont-want-god-youd-better-have-a-multiverse/

The only evidence some atheists/skeptics would accept would be of the sort that absolutely irresistibly compels belief. Just as it is impossible to doubt that the sun exists, they want it to be impossible to doubt that God exists. Only then they will believe.

Not all are as adamantly opposed to belief in God, but many are. But Christianity teaches a different kind of relationship with God, in which the believer relates to God through faith and love. In so doing the believer expresses a morally significant choice, not a compelled belief or behavior.

God is perfect in holiness and righteousness; those who love holiness and righteousness will seek him and know him (John 14:20). Those who hate it will hide from him. God makes it possible for us to choose either response, according to Christian teachings.

The Argument (First Part)

With that as background I begin to explore the following as an experimental series of thoughts:

1. Judaism and Christianity teach that God desires to make himself known to those whose hearts seek him.
2. Judaism and Christianity teach that God's self-revelation will be hidden from those who reject his holiness and righteousness.

   Therefore,

3. Knowledge of God is a matter of heart attitude as much as (or more than) evidences.
4. But Christianity teaches that God is creator and true; therefore his creation should give a true witness (evidences) concerning his reality.
5. Given (3) and (4), we should expect the world to provide evidence for God, but not to compel belief.

   Therefore,

127

6. We would expect God to have created a world in which evidences could be interpreted either as supporting or not supporting his existence.

7. Those who know God affirm that there are objective evidences to support their belief in his objective reality, and deny that purported evidences against God are decisive.

8. Those who deny God deny that those evidences count adequately for the existence of God, and/or affirm that evidences against God are decisive. BLIND — CHOICE

9. Based on (7) and (8), we see that the world is such that it is humanly possible to conclude either that God exists or he does not. Belief in God is not compelled by the evidences.

10. The world is such that the conditions in (5) and (6) are met.

11. The state of the evidence is consistent with Judeo-Christian teachings (1) through (6). The argument so far is a defeater for ebon musing's version of the *hiddenness* argument against God, and I think rather solid as far as it goes.

But there is more:

The Divine Hiddenness Argument *For* Christianity

1. The Judeo-Christian understanding of God in (1), (2), and (3) above was developed thousands of years ago.

2. The state of the evidence in (11), having persisted for centuries, it is remarkable for its *endurance*.

3. Both believers and unbelievers in God must acknowledge that no matter how strongly they hold to their own beliefs, thoughtful persons can hold to the opposite. Neither belief for nor against God is *compelled* by the evidence.

4. Thus (from the state of the evidence in (11) is also remarkably *fine-tuned*.

5. This persistence and fine-tuning are suggestive of an intelligent guiding intentionality ruling over them.

6. This guiding intentionality could only come from a personal God who has intended that state of affairs.

That's the argument in outline. Steps (1) through (11) are defensive: they answer and undercut a certain argument against God. In the second step of steps I attempt to go beyond that and show that God's "hiddenness" may hint at something more positive. I do not claim it as a proof for God; it is not that strong. But it is at least intriguing, and, as I have said, suggestive.

Issues and Questions

There are issues here for us to discuss. The oddity in this argument is that it uses perceived lack of evidence for God (8) as positive evidence for God. That would be an issue if this were an argument for some generic theism, but it is not; it is for the Christian God, who desires humans to be able rationally to believe yet not be compelled to believe. I believe the argument stands in that regard.

A second difficulty lies in the Christian doctrine of God's sovereignty over election of believers. I am going to name that as a potential problem and leave it as an item for your own reflection.

A third difficulty is that the final argument can be viewed as a member of a class of arguments that have failed spectacularly in other usages. Richard Dawkins once said, *"The universe that we observe has precisely the properties we should expect if there is, at bottom, no design, no purpose, no evil, no good, nothing but pitiless indifference."* Another atheist, Victor Stenger, has said, *"The laws of physics are just what they would be expected to be if they came from nothing."*

My argument here could be paraphrased, *"The world has just the properties we would expect if it were created by a God who wanted belief in him to be supported but not compelled by the evidences."*

Dawkins's and Stenger's arguments share this weakness: they propose that we know just how universes can be designed, that we have compared possible universes, and that we have discovered — eureka! — ours is just right for our preferred metaphysical position. It's unlikely that this kind of analysis is possible. My argument may share the same weakness. (Dawkins's and Stenger's arguments have other serious problems besides, but they are less relevant to the current discussion.)

Nevertheless, in spite of those potential weaknesses, I think it's remarkable that today, thousands of years after the formulation of Judeo-Christian views of God, we find ourselves still in a world where the evidences are fine-tuned the way they are. This fine-tuning is not objectively measurable the way the fine-tuning of physics and cosmology are. Still I think it is interesting and suggestive. It might even be positive evidence for a fine-tuner.

February 18, 2011

What Would it Take for Me to Give Up Belief in Jesus?

Here's a common skeptical challenge: "You believe no matter what. There isn't any possible fact or discovery that could ever cause you to change your mind. Which means you don't care about facts; your belief is disconnected from real data." This charge is related to a principle called "falsifiability" that's often used by scientists: "You can't call it true *unless you've tried and tested the ways it might have been* false *instead."*

So is it true that Christian belief is impervious to any possible facts? In this essay – if that's the right name for it – I've created a list of the major relevant facts the show how well Christianity fits with what we know about reality. To explain everything on these lists would take at least another book. My point here is simply to show how long the list is. Christianity really does fit with the facts of reality.

I pick it up here from the skeptical question.

Skeptics often ask, "Is there anything that could possibly cause you to give up your belief in Jesus Christ?"

It's a good question and a complicated one.

The good part is this: As Karl Popper explained, knowledge should be falsifiable in principle. If you hold a belief that can't be falsified under any imaginable circumstances, your belief might be disconnected from reality. If it wasn't true, how would you know it wasn't true? If you can't answer that question, then maybe you don't really know that it is true.

Should Christianity Be Falsifiable?

The complicated part is this. Falsifiability isn't a magic key that opens the door to all knowledge. The axioms of logic are true but they're not falsifiable, because falsification is a principle that can only work if the axioms of logic actually are true. You can't falsify logic without assuming logic is true. Mathematical facts like 2+2=4 aren't falsifiable in principle either, because they're just true.

Similarly, if Christianity is true, then falsifiability isn't predicted as part of its truth claims. That isn't slippery thinking; it's essential to Christianity's conception of God.

If it's true that God is God and Jesus Christ is his Son, born of a virgin, crucified and resurrected, then it's *comprehensively true*. God is the God of all reality. He created and has his imprint on everything. That includes all possible evidences, and even all the material a person could draw from to imagine God's non-existence. Skeptics imagine they can imagine a world without God, but they are deceived; they're using the materials God gave them to imagine he doesn't exist. If Christianity is true, it's unfalsifiable in principle.

So falsifiability is complicated, when judging whether Christianity is true. But I have an answer to the question, "what would it take for me to give up my belief?" anyway.

The Bones of Jesus?

It isn't the answer I hear from a lot of other Christians: "I would give up my faith if someone showed me the bones of Jesus Christ, proving he never rose from the dead." People who say that are probably sincere enough, but in actual practice it's no better than a dodge. We all know that if someone showed us "the bones of Jesus Christ," it would be easy to believe they were someone else's bones instead.

No, for me the answer is this: I would give up my Christian belief if someone showed me a better explanation for reality. Christianity provides a better foundation than any other worldview for explaining at least 50 facts that need explaining.

The Comprehensive Foundation/Explanation For:

The human condition

- Rationality

- Consciousness

- Meaning

- Purpose

- Our moral sense

- Our person-ness: that we are distinct individuals with real personality amidst others like us in that sense

- The persistence of identity and self-ness in human beings

- Our sense that we were meant to be better than we are

- Our millennia of failure to improve ourselves

- Our empirically obvious need for help if we are going to get better

- Our awareness of a spiritual dimension to reality

- Our persistent sense that there is more to life than what we can see here

The world around us

- The real existence of goodness

- The real existence of beauty

- The real lack of goodness and beauty, i.e., the existence of evil

- The rationality of existence (for example, nature's amenable to rational, scientific investigation)

- Unity within diversity

Complexity with purpose

- The universe's fitness for complex life

- Earth's fitness for complex life

- The origin of the first life

- The development of the species

- Earth's unique fitness in space and time for scientific discovery

History

- The Bible's existence as a unified library with a common theme spanning many, many generations

- The long existence of the Jewish people

- The early philosophical excellence of Judaic monotheism

- The uniqueness of the Genesis creation account with respect to all other creation accounts

- Archaeological discoveries confirming biblical data

- The perfect self-sacrificial goodness of Jesus Christ presented without flaw in four distinct narratives, unlike any other character in history or literature

- The set of broadly accepted historical facts surrounding the narrative of Jesus' resurrection

- The quick onset (within 3 to 5 years maximum) of Christian teachings regarding Jesus' resurrection

- The historical accuracy of writers such as Luke

- The conversion of Saul of Tarsus

- The wisdom of New Testament ethical teaching, in the Gospels and in Paul especially

- The countercultural value early Christians gave to women and children

- The successful rise of the Christian church despite strong opposition

- Christianity's unique contribution to world's understanding of compassion, human worth, and freedom

- Christianity's resilience over time: despite millennia of intellectual and social attack, it stands strong and remains (on some measures if not all) the world's fastest growing religion

Sociological and medical information

- The 99 factors/dimensions in which Christian teens showed healthier outcomes than non-believers, as reported in Christian Smith and Melanie Lundquist Denton, *Soul Searching: The Religious and Spiritual Lives of American Teenagers,* Oxford University Press, 2009.

- The much-lower divorce rate among Christians who attend church and pray together regularly

- The much-lower crime rate among Christians

- The multitude of other ways in which religious person exhibit better physical and mental health than nonbelievers

- The prevalence of credible, testable reports of miracles around the world

- The existence of credible, testable reports of the soul departing the body and returning again in near-death experiences

Personal experience

- The complete turnaround in my attitude toward life when I accepted Christ

- My sudden, massive increase in interest in the Bible at the same time

- The sense of freedom I've experienced in knowing there's forgiveness for my sins

- My turn away from self-centered goals to other-centered goals

- The love I experience from God in prayer

- The love I experience from other Christians — a love that's been tested in a wide variety of cross-cultural situations, including places where I've been interacting with people whose countries have been enemies of mine

- The miraculous prayer answers I've experienced

I could add more, but I think you get the picture.

If There Were a Better Explanation, I Could Possibly Give Up My Belief

I'm not saying that Christianity is the sole explanation for *any* of the above, but that it contributes *very strongly and positively* to explaining *all* of them. Again, I'm not saying that *none* of these is explainable on any other worldview, but only Christianity covers them *all*. Every other worldview I've encountered fails on several of them, if not most of them.

If someone offered me a better explanation for all these things, I'd consider that a good reason to reject Christianity. I doubt that's possible. I don't think God intended it to be possible.

November 16, 2016

Part 4: Intelligent Design vs. Naturalism

The Intelligent Design debate occupied a great deal of my energy for several years on *Thinking Christian*. It's coming back into view again in 2017 after a hiatus. While Intelligent Design isn't necessarily apologetics, it lines up closely with it in terms of a positive argument for God.

Young Earth, Old Earth, And Not Having To Know The Answer

There's a battle raging within Christianity. Maybe you've encountered it, maybe not. I run into it all the time. It's a fight over how we should interpret the first chapters of Genesis in light of scientific opinion on the how the universe came to be – but especially when the universe came to be. Some say it all happened within the last 10,000 years or so, others say the science can be trusted and it was over 13 billion years ago. The battle is unfortunately bitter in some places. In this essay I offer an answer that promotes both peace and biblical and intellectual integrity.

Some time ago at the Evangelical Philosophical Society conference I ran across a pair of exhibit booths, placed judiciously distant from each other, promoting two different views of creation. One was for a young-earth creation society, the other for an old-earth group (YEC and OEC, respectively).

I talked with the people manning both booths. The YEC group was convinced that the OEC people were tossing out belief in Scripture. The OEC rep was quite sure the YEC folks were destroying Christian credibility. These views are typical, not just at that conference but throughout all debate on the topic. It's acrimonious and unpleasant. There's got to be a better answer. And there is. I learned it as an undergrad. It's stood the test of time.

College Debates
I was a music major at Michigan State University in the mid–1970s. "Creation science" writings by Morris and Whitcomb were attracting a lot of attention then, even among us music majors. One of my fellow Christians in the music department, a bassoonist named Will, was the son of an MSU professor of biology (or

possibly geology, I don't remember for sure). The debate was especially tough on him, since he was torn between his dad's science and what others were telling him he had to believe as a Christian.

We all had a lot to sort out, or so we thought. We were all looking at competing claims about radiometric dating, dust on the moon (that was a live question at the time), and how a catastrophic flood might or might not have affected the surface of the earth.

Not Having To Know It All

Then one day it struck me: "I'm not a geologist, paleontologist, biologist, or cosmologist. I'm not an Ancient Near East literature specialist, equipped to interpret Genesis in literary and cultural context. I'm a music major! Why should I have to decide?"

I've been told since then that I should be able to look at the first chapters of Genesis and know how to interpret them. Not really. There are technical questions that take at least some specialized knowledge to judge. I've always been struck, for example, by the poetic structure and style displayed by Genesis 1. Poetry is often meant to be taken figuratively. As an undergrad I wondered whether this might mean it was intended as figurative language.

I wasn't doubting that we should treat the text as trustworthy and authoritative; rather, I wasn't sure I knew how the text was intended to be interpreted. It seemed to me that was a question for Old Testament scholars and Ancient Near East specialists — not for trombonists.

That's when I gave myself permission to say, "I don't know, and that's okay." It was tremendously freeing. About fifteen years later I ran across Hugh Ross's *The Fingerprint of God: Recent Scientific Discoveries Reveal the Unmistakable Identity of the Creator* (the link is to an updated edition). It was the first old-earth creation book I had read. Again, it included science outside my own expertise, but it reinforced for me a sense of permission to suspend judgment on the question. Because I'm not an expert, and on this topic I don't see any requirement that I should be one. It's okay not to decide.

Hard Questions Don't Have Easy Answers

This has absolutely nothing with being hesitant to take a stand with Scripture. I live to promote its truth and I'll die standing for its truths, if need be.

God said it would take diligence and work, though, for us to rightly handle his word of truth (2 Timothy 2:15). There's no guarantee in the Lord that all truths should be accessible right on the surface.

Of course, I've always been confident that *chance* was not in charge of origins; *God* was. I have always been convinced there was an original human couple created in God's image, originally innocent, who fell into sin and death through disobedience, pretty much the way it's outlined in Genesis 1 through 3. I could explain why I am sure of these things; but I don't want to stray from my point, which is this: We know a lot, but we don't have to have know everything.

Two Books of Revelation

Yet the Bible is not our only source of truth. Theologians say it this way: God wrote two books: the book of Scripture and the book of nature. Both books need to be interpreted (or rightly handled, one might say). Both books are susceptible to being interpreted either rightly or wrongly.

The Bible is more personal, more revelational, more propositional, more accessible, and therefore superior in multiple ways to the book of nature. But we still need to interpret passages like Genesis in context of all God's revelation, including the rest of Scripture, God's self-revelation in nature.

We also need to interpret these passages, like all language, in the literary and historical setting in which they were first composed. There is a reason we turn to commentaries to learn about the situation in which the Bible's books were written. The context and content of Genesis 1 and 2 are (obviously) the most distant and distinctive of any passage in Scripture. Many questions remain open, as far as I can see.

Some questions are difficult, technical, and contentious even among specialists. Christians who love the Lord and believe the Bible disagree on many things — modes of baptism, for example — and yet we can still have fellowship with each other. Likewise, godly men and women who love the Lord and trust the truth of God's *two books* of revelation don't always agree on what they mean with respect to creation, and still have fellowship together.

Bad Policy

It's okay not to know the answer to complex technical questions. Why, then, do so many YEC believers take dogmatic stands, based on short pamphlets or quick web pages they've read about errors in radiometric dating or some other old-earth objection? Deciding difficult, technically involved issues that way is bad policy. Deciding for YEC that way would be bad policy even if everyone someday decided YEC was right.

Earlier this year, a young-earth creation society invited me to raft the Grand Canyon and see (among other things) how its features could be explained by the Flood. Man, would I have loved the adventure! But I declined.

I told them, "I am not a geologist today, and I'm not qualified to judge the arguments for and against your position. If I took this rafting trip, I would still not be a geologist, and I would be, if anything, less qualified to judge the merits of your position, for I doubt I would be getting a balanced view on it."

It's bad policy to think we could know hard answers to hard questions even after a week of study. What's a week, after all? How long is a Ph.D. program?

It's Okay To Say We Don't Know
I'm all for study and learning, advancing our understanding of science, Scripture, and all of life. I'm totally in favor of being confident in what we really do know. Claiming we know more than we do, however, does not advance the truth, it undermines it. It's an act of intellectual dishonesty toward oneself, and it damages our credibility with others.

Mystery is not a bad thing either for worship or for science. God's ways exceed our understanding — what a great reason for worship! The world is full of unanswered questions — what a great motivation for study! So please, let's give ourselves the freedom to say we don't know.

Closing Questions:
This will probably raise several questions. I can only acknowledge them briefly; I can't deal with them here at length.

1. Is there anything at all that Christians can know about creation as non-specialists?

2. Do I have any opinion at all on the age of the universe?

3. How far does the principle of "I don't know, and I don't have to know," extend?

4. Does that principle undermine all non-specialist biblical knowledge?

5. Am I saying that Christians are more guilty of false confidence than others?

My answers to questions 1, 2, are both yes. To 4 and 5 I would answer no. The third question doesn't have a short answer.

They're all important questions, but I am leaving them otherwise unanswered for now. This article is intended to emphasize one central point, and if I were to lay out my full position on those matters it would dilute that one point I'm really hoping to make here.

November 22, 2010

What's Wrong and What's Right
with Intelligent Design

There's a movement among some scientists and thinkers called "Intelligent Design." It's built on the idea that nature shows us it's more reasonable to think the world and everything in it came about by the work of an intelligent designer. It's an extremely controversial viewpoint. Most academic scientists resist it strongly (at least in public).

The science of Intelligent Design doesn't tell us who that Designer must be. That's actually a strength of the movement, as I show below. But still there are things that must be true of this Designer. In this essay I show how those "things that must be true" actually help explain why some people resist the idea of a designer.

I had a powerful "aha moment" one night some time ago. I believe I actually felt the deep emotional revulsion feel ID opponents have toward Intelligent Design (ID). I was reading Thomas Woodward's *Darwin Strikes Back*. I think it was a kind of gifting moment, through which I was able to take on the other side's perspective and gain new insight. I was reading the following passage on the Cambrian Explosion, which was a period during which (according to the fossil record) many thousands of new species suddenly appeared in a short period of geological time, about 530 million years ago. Woodward writes,

> The name 'explosion' is used widely in the literature of professional paleontology in describing this dramatic fossil debut.... where we find not just gaps between slightly different forms but fossil chasms between different phyla that abruptly appear in the rocks....The Cambrian gaps are persisting [in spite of new fossil finds]; with a defiance and stubbornness that is now legendary. What's worse, those chasms are not

just enduring; they are steadily increasing in number through discoveries of new bizarre creatures... in recent decades.

ID theorists point to the Cambrian explosion as evidence that gradualistic evolution doesn't, and cannot, explain the fossil record.

Now, this was not new information to me, but it somehow struck me this time just how this must appear to some people. Here we have something like 200,000 species among the fossils, most of which arrived suddenly 530 million years ago and are now gone. ID (usually) says that each one of them, or at least each group or "kind," required a special intervention to appear as a new species.

But what kind of an intelligence would do *that*? Why would this intelligence build up to these new species with a series of simpler forms, most of which are also gone now? Why would this intelligence create a dinosaur world that's now been wiped away? I believe I have a sense now (though I still don't agree, as I'll explain later) of what some people say when they consider this intelligence as some kind of fictional bumbler mucking about in the world, creating in fits and starts, not getting it right for the longest time. It's so much more pleasing — especially to our Western consciousness — to think of things coming and going through natural processes over a period of time.

What Kind of Intelligence?

So then, what kind of intelligence would do that? It's a good question. Intelligent Design theorists say they are making an *inference to the best explanation:* that we can draw a valid analogy from our everyday experience, which shows us that information and design always originate from intelligence, to some kind of intelligence behind the natural order. But why stop there? I wonder if it's really possible to do as ID theorists do, which is to start from the natural evidence, and reason from there to bare intelligence. I don't think it's entirely wrong — in fact, it's correct in a very powerful way. I'll come back to that in a moment.

Mysterious

For now, though, I'm suggesting that we shouldn't stop there. Why just reason to the conclusion that there's *intelligence* there? Ought we not at least also reason to *mystery?* For if there is something analogous to human intelligence there, there is also something about it that is very hard to understand. It's a theory of *Mysterious* Intelligence.

Profligately Creative

Then, as we continue to puzzle over why this intelligence would develop all those thousands of creatures, there seems to be another important analogy we could safely draw. When we see new people building things being built for no apparent purpose, it's usually the result of some creative impulse. Art doesn't have to have a purpose, other than to delight the beholder. In the case of natural history, if the creative impulse is part of the explanation, it seems playful and wasteful at the same time, or *profligate*. This mysterious, creative intelligence has resources to spare, and no compunction about using them. This seems to be leading us to a richer theory than simple ID; it's a theory of Mysterious, *Profligately Creative* Intelligence.

Highly Involved Outsider

But not just that. This intelligence seems likely not to be part of the natural world, yet it intervenes here. The world of the Cambrian explosion was stepped into frequently from outside. It's haunted by this other-worldly intelligence. Otherwise, how would these 200,000 or so new species have arisen? So we seem to be moving toward a theory of Mysterious, Profligately Creative, *Highly Involved Outsider* Intelligence.

Purposeful and Powerful

Finally, we might as well recognize that just about every ID theorist speaks of purpose, and great power is assumed; so we're talking about a *Purposeful, Powerful*, Mysterious, Profligately Creative, Highly Involved Outsider Intelligence

Anathema!

This is nothing but anathema to modern man. A Purposeful, Powerful, Mysterious, Profligately Creative, Highly Involved Intelligent Outsider simply *does not belong in our mindset.* No wonder ID draws so much fire! We're all naturalists to some extent. Even we who believe in God are so highly influenced by the scientific mindset, it's hard to shake free of it for even a moment. African or Pacific Island tribes they may see spirits in every tree and rock — we see atoms and molecules and energy, and we know how they interact. We know what's really going on, and it's not spooks. This is the problem with Intelligent Design. ID's opponents keep pushing ID's proponents to name the intelligence we're talking about. We're shy to do that from the scientific perspective, but this Mysterious Creative Outsider haunts every mention of ID.

Aesthetic/Emotional Objections

Now here's the interesting thing, though: if you've been watching this debate, you've noticed that if there's an objection to this kind of Intelligence, it's mostly emotional or aesthetic: We dare not countenance such a possibility, because it just doesn't fit the way we have thought the world is and we don't like it.

There are rational arguments along those lines too, but they're nothing new, nothing that ID hasn't already dealt with from the philosophical side of its efforts. But this feeling of strangeness exposes more clearly what ID is about. It's not about bare intelligence: it's about *Purposeful, Powerful, Mysterious, Profligately Creative, Highly Involved Outsider Intelligence.* From my perspective as a Christian, it's about God.

The World Is Not So Immune to Intervention as We Think

At this point I must step aside from the subject slightly for a moment to speak of something that makes matters better in some ways and worse in others. Phillip Jenkins was Distinguished Professor of Religious Studies and History at Penn State when he

150

wrote that the most under-reported, and possibly the most significant social movement in the entire world in the 20th Century, was the global rise of Christianity, especially south of the Equator, in Asia, and in Muslim countries.

J.P. Moreland quotes credible research showing that in the last 30 years of the century, serious Christians increased worldwide by a factor of 10, and the number of Muslims coming to faith in Christ in the last few decades is greater than in all previous history combined.[10] Much of this explosion is fueled by miracles: dreams, vision, healings and the like. These things are credibly reported in sources like the Washington *Post* and the Orange County *Register* [the links have expired since this was first posted].

It seems that the world is not so immune to intervention by an intelligent outsider as we have thought. Maybe we Westerners are wrong about some things. (And maybe, as Moreland says at the end of that talk, it's happening more in our part of the world than we've recognized.)

But the scientist says, "If God is doing this all the time, how can there be any such thing as science? If God is always intervening — *interfering* — how can we count on any regularity anywhere? Yet, clearly we can! So this does not add up." That question is actually not so hard. Part of God's intention in doing these things is to communicate himself to people.

If he were always interfering, such that there was no such thing as a reliable natural order, there could be no communication in it. It's a signal-to-noise ratio thing. God's communication has to be different from the regularities of the world if it's to be actual communication; thus there must be regularities. Those regularities define the way we usually experience the world, and God's interventions to change that order are rare exceptions.

---

10   See http://www.strcast2.org/podcast/weekly/021906.m3u

Aspects of God's character enter in here that I don't know how to derive as an inference from nature. Biblical believers know him as good, trustworthy, and faithful. To the extent that ID is intimating a Powerful Outsider whose goodness and faithfulness unknown, however, I can see how that would be just opening a conceptual door to chaos.

The Weakness Summarized: An Affront and An Assault

That, as I said, was somewhat of an aside, for I started out talking about ID from an empirical perspective, and then I looked at divine intervention from a theological perspective. The two views unite in this: The whole idea is an affront to the mindset of a universally predictable, controllable, regular, universal, natural reality. It's a terrible assault on philosophical naturalism (PN, the idea that there is no reality except matter and energy and law and chance).

That's the emotional impact. *But the emotional effect of this does not mean it's not true.* Lurking behind ID is what I would call PPMPCHIOID: *Purposeful, Powerful, Mysterious, Profligately Creative, Highly Involved Outsider Intelligent Design.* Opponents accuse ID of being disingenuous when it says it makes no claims, other than intelligence, regarding the identity of the designer it seeks. But don't we all have PPMPCHIOID — or God — in mind? Isn't ID being dishonest when it denies this?

The Weakness Is a Strength

I don't think so. In fact, this apparent weakness of ID is also its strength. It offers so little about the Designer it seeks; but it does not try to offer more than its tools allow. To look for Design, signifying purposeful intelligence, is something we can do from within the empirical sciences. To look for the rest of it is beyond the reach of science.

We have conceptual tools for identifying purposeful design in nature. Yes, I know this is the very point that's most in controversy. There seems to be at least one such tool that is to be universally accepted, though: Michael Behe's irreducible complexity (IC). Many scientists have taken Behe to task over this, but in very specific ways. They've said that his examples of IC are not really irreducible, or they have doubted that instances of IC in nature can really be proven. They have not (to my knowledge) ever credibly denied that IC — if reliably identified — signals the action of intelligence. So we have at least that one conceptual tool, going back all the way to Darwin himself.

I believe William Dembski's complex specified information (CSI) is also a strong indicator of intelligence, as is the origin of biological information, as discussed by Stephen Meyer in _Signature in the Cell_.

But we don't have empirically-based, scientific tools identifying and discriminating other features of the designer, like his faithfulness, his desire to communicate, his love, and so on. At least, we can't identify those things directly. So when an empirical research program says it's only trying to identify intelligence, it is being both careful and honest. (It is not thereby trying to sneak God into the public schools.) It is trying to do just what it can conceivably do through its tools.

What's Right and Wrong
What's both wrong and right about ID, then, is its bare minimalist claim of looking for purposeful intelligence in a designer of life. It is right in looking only for what it has the conceptual tools to potentially find. That there may be a PPMPCHIOID — an active creator God — lurking there raises all kinds of emotional reactions, which I think I understand better now. It's hard to like ID if you don't like the idea of a God being involved in the natural order.

And it's really hard to like ID if you see it as a way to sneak God back into American public education. That's the other rampant conspiracy theory surrounding ID. Plain statements of facts from ID leaders don't seem to have lessened fears of this.

To repeat those plain statements: as a scientific research program, ID is a minimalist theory, seeking only to identify instances of purposeful design in nature. Its educational agenda is even more minimalist: ID leaders aren't trying to get ID taught in the public schools. (It's been said a thousand times.) We're only asking for a more complete accounting of evolution to be presented, including empirical challenges facing it. That's all. How evil is that?

Not much, in my view. For those who are guided by an emotional response guiding them, though, it's convenient to distort ID into something other than what it is; saying it's a religious and political campaign. ID has to clear that rhetorical hurdle every time it meets public opinion.

But I don't want to get sidetracked there. Instead I want to give proper credence to the emotional and aesthetic challenge ID presents to people of a naturalistic mindset. As I said, I've had a taste of that feeling, and it's powerful. It doesn't determine the truth of ID, but we have to recognize it as a significant and real part of this controversy's landscape, and treat it with respect.

April 16, 2010

Who's Drawing Evidence-Free Conclusions Now?

*People who resist Intelligent Design like to say that there's no
real evidence for it. In this essay I show that the main opposing
view has no need for evidence itself. Many scientists start from a
position called naturalism: They're convinced there is no God, no
spiritual reality, no intelligence designing reality. If any such thing
exists, it doesn't actually do anything in our world.*

*I say that if you start with that naturalistic belief, you pretty much
have to conclude that evolution is true. You have no other choice
— except to give up your belief that the world is strictly natural.
Which too many people are reluctant to do. So they're forced to
fit the evidence into their beliefs, rather than letting the evidence
guide their conclusions.*

*This essay is on the more technical side, so please take it for
what it's worth to you.*

Reading the National Academy of Sciences book on *Science,
Evolution, and Creationism*, I was struck by the fact that there's
nothing like real evidence anywhere for naturalistic evolution.
That is, one cannot validly conclude, just from evidence in nature,
that everything can be explained only and exclusively in terms of
natural causes and effects. There is always a background perspective.

How, for example, does one treat the incomplete fossil record?
Do we see *Tiktaalik* (discovered in 2004 in northern Canada, with
features combining those of fish and of four-legged animals) as a
strong confirmation that land animals evolved out of the sea? Or
do we ask why, of all the millions of transitional forms there must
have been over the eons, so terribly few have been found? If transitional forms are like rafts for a swimmer across a sea, do we pay
more attention to the few rafts or the long water?

155

But for science (or some scientists, at least), only one perspective is allowed in the debate. As the NAS book said, "In science, explanations must be based on naturally occurring phenomena."

There's a huge problem with this. It's a scientific problem, actually. You see, the NAS's naturalistic position can only lead to one conclusion, but it's a position (and therefore a conclusion) that *precedes the evidence* rather than following from the evidence.

Conclusions Are Always Colored by Presuppositions

To put it another way: how we interpret the evidences of natural history is inevitably colored by the presuppositions we bring in to the question with us. The NAS position is functionally one of ontological materialism (also known as philosophical materialism, or philosophical naturalism). That view is best summarized as, Nothing exists except for matter and energy, and their interactions according to a law-like regularity.

Admittedly, the NAS book doesn't go so far as saying there is nothing but natural phenomena, but it only admits natural phenomena into discussion. But even this is not a position that flows out of science or out of the evidence; it is a position by which one interprets science.

Different Starting Points

Everybody starts with some opinion on these philosophical and theological issues. The following chart shows how different initial viewpoints will color one's interpretations.

This chart only works from top to bottom, not in reverse. It's not about the metaphysical position one derives from one's beliefs about nature; it's about the beliefs one is bound to derive from nature based on one's metaphysical beliefs. In other words, the point I'm making here is that metaphysics, not scientific evidence, can drive people to certain beliefs, even some that they'll insist are "scientific."

156

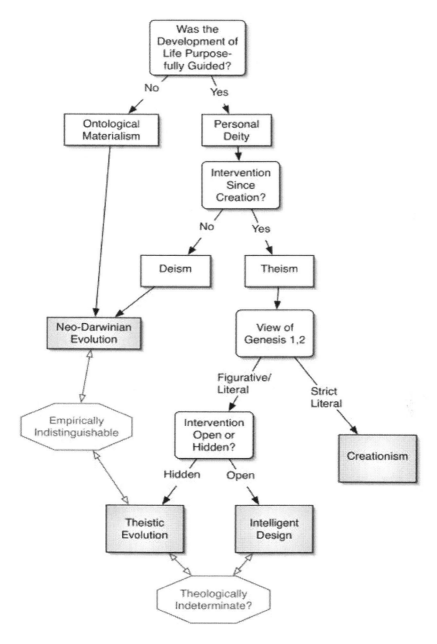

(There's some partial overlap between ID and Young-Earth Creation, but including that would have made the chart more unwieldy.)

The Starting Point: *Could* Life's Development Have Been Purposefully Guided?

Much of the debate on ID centers on whether it's credible even to consider the possibility that the development of life has been purposefully guided. That's where this chart begins. Those who say "no" are ontological materialists/naturalists: they are convinced that nothing at the ground of existence (ontology) has purpose or can act as a guiding agent; all there is, is matter and energy and their interactions.

Not "What will be will be

The only option on the table for materialists is Neo-Darwinian Evolution and/or its intellectual descendants. That's it. There are no other options on the table for them. They are bound by their prior metaphysical commitments to conclude, "It's evolution!" no matter what evidence they look at. That's a little fishy, as I'll explain further, below.

Belief in purposeful guidance, on the other hand, is typically tied to belief in a personal God. God's guidance may conceivably have been entirely contained in "seed" form from the moment of creation, such that God has not intervened since then. This is a generally *deistic* view, which leads also to conclusions a whole lot like Neo-Darwinism, though its assumptions may not be as strictly materialistic as those of many neo-Darwinians.

Options for Theists

Theists have more options. Among those (including myself) who believe in a personal God who intervenes (the theistic view), some are *young-earth creationists* who view Genesis 1 as being true in the plainest literal sense.

Others view Genesis 1 as not being literally true in that sense; most of these hold what I call the figurative/literal view. (See the

158

chapter "Young Earth, Old Earth, And Not Having to Know the Answer" for more on that.) Thus there are those who believe in a personal God who may have intervened in the development of life since creation, and who do not ascribe to the young-earth view.

This group may further divide into two sub-groups, based on their theology or their view of the evidences. The determining question at this stage is one's answer to the question, was God's intervention hidden, or is it discoverable? Theistic evolution believes God was present and involved in the development of life, but his work was hidden, perhaps even tucked away on a quantum level, so that we will not discover his intervention through empirical means.

Then there is Intelligent Design theism, comprising those who believe that God's intervention left traces that scientists can discern today.

(Remember where this flow chart begins and how it progresses. It leads to a theistic version of Intelligent Design, but that does not mean that all ID is theistic. ID research that begins with empirical evidences in nature leads from there *toward intelligence* as a conclusion, but not toward God. (See the chapter "What's Wrong and What's Right with Intelligent Design" for more on that.)

Drawing Conclusions
The first octagonal box on the chart points out that Neo-Darwinism and theistic evolution are empirically indistinguishable. *There is no science that can discern between God being absent or having just hidden his interventions.*

This contributes to answering whether evolution science and religion are necessarily incompatible. They are not, if this box represents any possible reality. Neither can disprove the other, so neither need view the other as enemy. It also demonstrates that atheistic evolutionists like Dawkins, Dennett, Wilson, etc. have not arrived at their dogmatic atheism through evolutionary science (as they claim) but through other prejudices. Their position is not determined by the evidences.

The second octagonal box asks whether there is any theological need to choose between ID and a form of theistic evolutionism. The question mark is there for a reason. Theistic evolutionists see their position as compatible with the Bible Young-earth creationists strenuously object. [A recent ID-oriented volume, *Theistic Evolution: A Scientific, Philosophical, and Theological Critique* repeats that objection, though in markedly different terms.]

Evidence-Free?

Here's the really interesting point I want to close with, though: Theists have options. We can let our conclusions be guided by the evidence. Naturalists can't. They can only choose Neo-Darwinism (or its descendants), regardless of any evidence that might come forward.

So I ask you, who's more likely to draw evidence-free conclusions?

*This discussion is not intended to cover all options exhaustively. It's focused on the major players in the debate. I've left out the impersonal pantheistic and polytheistic views of deity, which don't seem to be involved in the discussion. Pantheists (or panentheists) of the New Age variety typically land in the Neo-Darwinian camp anyway, and other eastern religions do not seem to propose creation stories with any real attempt at credibility. I'm not qualified to speak on their views, at any rate, nor am I qualified to speak on the Muslim form of theism. Panspermia is not included here because it seems to be another version of the ontological materialist view, and this is more about the development of life than its initial origins on earth anyway.

January 14, 2008

Evolution's "Otherwise Practical Polyamory"

Is it harmful to believe in evolution? Some scoff at the idea that it could be so. They say it's a scare tactic used to bully people into believing the Bible instead of science. But if you believe in anything like standard morality, you'll find in this essay that there really is something dangerous about believing in evolution.

Evolution — the naturalistic kind that denies God completely — is dangerous. Seriously and without exaggeration. I've never seen its danger exposed so clearly as in Jesse Bering's article at Scientific American's website, "Polyamory chic, gay jealousy, and the evolution of a broken heart" (caution: crude language).[11] He writes,

> There's a strange whiff in the media air, a sort of polyamory chic in which liberally minded journalists, an aggregate mass of anti-religious pundits and even scientists themselves have begun encouraging readers and viewers to use evolutionary theory to revisit and revise their sexual attitudes and, more importantly, their behaviors in ways that fit their animal libidos more happily. ...

> The basic logic is that, because human beings are not naturally monogamous but rather have been explicitly designed by natural selection to seek out ... ˜extra-pair copulatory partners ... having sex with someone other than your partner or spouse for the replicating sake of one's mindless genes... then suppressing these deep mammalian instincts is futile and, worse, is an inevitable death knell for an otherwise honest and healthy relationship.

---

[11]   https://blogs.scientificamerican.com/bering-in-mind/polyamory-chic-gay-jealousy-and-the-evolution-of-a-broken-heart/

If you believe, as I do, that we live in a natural rather than a supernatural world, then there is no inherent, divinely inspired reason to be sexually exclusive to one's partner. If you and your partner want to … [multiple suggested acts, omitted for reasons of decency] … then by all means do so (and take pictures). … Right is irrelevant. There is only what works and what doesn't work, within context, in biologically adaptive terms.

This is bound to provoke revulsion in any decent reader, and rightly so. Anger, too — rightly so. Even fear — again, rightly so. But not the kind of fear that some have mistakenly ascribed to some of us, like Stuart Kauffman, who wrote earlier this year,

> I suspect the fear of evolution is also based in the view of many that God is the author of our moral laws. Then if the Bible is God's literal word, and yet evolution is true, the Bible, the very word of God, is false, and our morality falls to the ground. …

> But evolution, in fact, is no enemy of morality.[12]

Or Michael Shermer, who wrote in the blurb for his book, *Why Darwin Matters*,

> Evolution happened, and the theory describing it is one of the most well founded in all of science. Then why do half of all Americans reject it? There are religious reasons, such as the fear of atheism and the perceived loss of ultimate meaning; there are psychological reasons, such as the ego-deflating realization that we are mere animals; and there are political reasons, such as the equation of evolution with moral relativism on the right, and the connection of evolution to eugenics and social Darwinism on the left.

---

12   http://www.npr.org/blogs/13.7/2010/01/intelligent_design_no_darwinia.html

This is of course sadly ironic in view of the metaphysical reasons many insist evolution must be true (see the chapter "Who's Drawing Evidence-Free Conclusions Now?")

Appropriate Fear

But that's an aside. No, this is not "I'm-afraid-of-evolution-therefore-I-can't-accept-it's-true." In fact, I reject naturalistic evolution because it is incoherent, impossible, and contradictory to other things I know to be true. The fear of evolution of which I speak is based on a reasoned knowledge of its actual dangers.

Some readers will jump in and say it's weak for me to be motivated by fear. I have a story about that. Last summer my wife and I encountered rattlesnakes on three consecutive hikes. It's never happened to me before. The first one was just off the path, it was a little one, and we stopped and took a picture of it.

The second one was stretched out fully across the path in our way. I chucked some stones toward it and waited till it slithered out of the way; then we walked on by.

The third one we heard but did not see. Other hikers ahead of us on the trail could see it on the far side of a shrub. We heard it rattling. I asked, "Is it coiled?" They said it was. Now, that was intriguing to me. I've never seen a coiled-up rattler in the wild. But we hightailed it out of there anyway. Fear of the second snake caused us to move slowly. Fear of the third one, coiled and ready to strike, drove us away completely. *To act based on fear of genuine danger is both good and wise.*

Ideas have consequences, and in the case of evolution, one of those consequences is that (as Bering said), "Right is irrelevant." That's a perfectly sound conclusion from naturalistic evolutionary premises. Do you think *that idea* has no consequences? Would you marry someone who believes right is irrelevant? Would you let your daughter date someone like that? If so, your lack of fear is a morally and intellectually reprehensible lack of wisdom.

Practical Polyamory?

Bering thinks he can get past all that. In spite of the "polyamory chic" of which he speaks at first, he goes on to say evolution gives us something to hold relationships together in something like sexual faithfulness:

> And that is simply the fact that we've evolved to empathize with other people's suffering, including the suffering of the people we'd betray by putting our affable genitals to their evolved promiscuous use.

> Heartbreak is every bit as much a psychological adaptation as is the compulsion to have sex with those other than our partners, and it throws a monster of a monkey wrench into the evolutionists' otherwise practical polyamory.

"Practical polyamory!" Do I fear sexuality being taught that way? Of course I do. What kind of idiot wouldn't? It's a coiled snake — even if there's empathy in the evolutionary mix.

Bering goes on to describe heartbreak in both social and chemical detail, include his own despair after being rejected by his gay lover.

> All this is to say that I reacted the way I did because, at an unconscious level, I didn't want my testiculared partner getting impregnated by another man. I don't consciously think of him as a woman, mind you; in fact, if I did, I assure you I wouldn't be with him. But tell that to my gonads and amygdalae.

His heart was broken. There's only one reason we don't do that to each other every chance we get: empathy. That's what Bering says holds human morality together.

Empathy's Limits

By no means would I diminish the value of empathy. It certainly does guide and restrain human behavior. When I wash the dishes or fold laundry at home, it's not because I love those jobs, but because I love my wife, and out of empathy I prefer that she not have to do them. Obviously, empathy informs much larger decisions as well. Of course, empathy is better explained on theism than naturalism. For Bering and other naturalistic evolutionists, however, empathy is a chimera, genetic self-interest masquerading as selflessness.

Empathy dances a dialectical *pas de deux* with promiscuous sexuality, a duet with (pardon the anthropomorphism) just one purpose: to produce multiple generations of babies. They're equal partners in their evolutionary art, says Bering, and together they perform very well.

There can be no right or wrong in that. It is what it is. It propagates genes. There's no logically defensible way to identify one partner in this dance as morally better than the other. They're both behaviors adapted for species survival, and neither could do it without the other. If you label empathy more respectable or praiseworthy than rape or wanton promiscuity, your labeling it so is just another behavior evolution has cooked up to join the dance. (It's more of a *pas de trois*.)

Oh, and one more thing: it's not your dance. "Tell that to my gonads and amygdalae," Bering says. He knows that evolution means he's a puppet on their string. If you *think* it's your dance — that you're anything but a puppet toy in the propagation game — that's another labeling behavior that evolution has found effective to get us all to reproduce.

I despise that teaching — even though it makes perfectly good sense on naturalistic assumptions. Because even though Bering thinks nothing can speak to his gonads and amygdalae, I know that people actually can think about their behaviors, and based on thinking they can actually make choices. I can see that if young people are taught a pervasive philosophical system that denies the roots of right and wrong, and that glorifies procreation, they'll decide to do exactly what they're doing. Hooking up at every chance they get. Cohabiting. Practicing serial marriage, divorcing right and left. Glorifying immorality of all sorts, both hetero- and homosexual.

And killing themselves emotionally, physically, and spiritually in the process.

August 25, 2010

Part 5: Answering the Skeptics

Positive arguments for God aren't enough; the skeptics challenges must be met as well. The "negative apologetics" (see the introduction to part 3) in this section address three common sets of skeptical confusions: the nature of Christianity, the supposedly materialistic nature of reality, and the meaning of "faith" in Christian practice.

"Christians Believe in Magic," or, Why Think, When Slogans Are So Much Less Work?

Atheists and skeptics often say Christians believe in magic. It's a thoroughly confused accusation — either that, or it's dishonest — yet they use it anyway. It's a great example of using slogans in place of actual thinking.

Atheists and skeptics often say Christians believe in magic. It's a thoroughly confused accusation — either that, or it's dishonest — yet they use it anyway. It's a great example of sloganeering instead of thinking. I'll come back to that at the end, under "the moral of the story." First, though, we need to look at the truth about Christianity and magic.

Defining "Magic"

I looked up several definitions in online dictionaries. Dictionary.com defines the noun form of "magic" as

1. the art of producing illusions as entertainment by the use of sleight of hand, deceptive devices, etc.; legerdemain; conjuring: *to pull a rabbit out of a hat by magic.*

2. the art of producing a desired effect or result through the use of incantation or various other techniques that presumably assure human control of supernatural agencies or the forces of nature. ...

3. the use of this art: *Magic, it was believed, could drive illness from the body.*

4. the effects produced: *the magic of recovery.*

5. power or influence exerted through this art: *a wizard of great magic.*

At Merriam-Webster we read "magic" as

1 a : — the use of means (as charms or spells) believed to have supernatural power over natural forces

1 b : magic rites or incantations

2 a : an extraordinary power or influence seemingly from a supernatural source

2 b : something that seems to cast a spell : enchantment

3:    the art of producing illusions by sleight of hand

The Oxford dictionaries define the word's adjectival form,

> used in magic or working by magic; having or apparently having supernatural powers: *a magic wand* [attributive] very effective in producing results, especially desired ones: *confidence is the magic ingredient needed to spark recovery*

"Magic" Applied to God, Prayer, Miracles

That pretty much covers the territory as far as dictionaries go. (Other reliable sources don't say much different.) Now the question is, which of these applies to Christian belief concerning God, prayer, or miracles? Entertainment magic certainly doesn't; everyone knows it's pure illusion.

My son is a street magician. He says magicians are the most honest people in the world: they let you know they're going to fool you and then they go ahead and do it. The word "magic" used metaphorically — *the magic of her smile* — has nothing to do with it either, obviously.

This Magic?

So the answer to our question seems rather to lie in one or more of these, which I'm re-numbering here for convenience:

1. The art of producing a desired effect or result through the use of incantation or various other techniques that presumably assure human control of supernatural agencies or the forces of nature.

2. The use of means (as charms or spells) believed to have supernatural power over natural forces

3. An extraordinary power or influence seemingly from a supernatural source

4. Having or apparently having supernatural powers

No, Not This Magic

If the question is whether God himself is magic (or a belief in God is a belief in magic), then number 1 and 2 are ruled out. No Christian believes God uses means, incantations, or techniques. No orthodox Christian believes that prayer is a matter of assuming (much less *assuring*) human control over God or the supernatural.

(Some name-it-and-claim-it Christians brush dangerously close to that belief, but to the extent they do so they depart from belief in the God of the Bible.)

Similarly, prayer is never thought, in Christianity, to contain or produce any sort of power over natural or supernatural forces. Rather it is a personal request to God that he would influence natural forces in a desired direction.

Yes, Christians often say there is power in prayer, but that's shorthand, an abbreviated reminder that there is power in God himself, and that he has promised to answer prayer according to his own will and his grace. The power is not in the prayer but in God himself.

Making Crucial Distinctions

These distinctions are crucial. The brief definitions I've quoted here are echoed and expanded in more technical literature: Magic, properly understood, is an attempt to take control of the supernatural by use of arcane techniques, or else it is some effect or power associated with such practices.

Some Christians may believe that there is such a thing as magic that genuinely meets that definition, but they ascribe its effect to the deceit of demons, and they reject it resoundingly.

If this kind of magic exists, which I personally doubt, it's only *apparently* the exercise of power over supernatural forces. Demons may play that game: they don't mind it at all, as long as they can ensnare souls.

As I said, I doubt this is real. My friend André Kole is a master illusionist (stage magician) who has traveled the world looking for any real magic of this sort. He goes where scientists have been baffled and have left, saying "there's no explanation for this." He says the problem with scientists is that they're trained to study what's true. To track an illusion takes an illusionist.

In his book *Miracles or Magic* he exposes psychic surgeons in the Philippines, levitating gurus in India, and so on: it's all illusion, trickery of the same sort used by entertainers on stage. So is God magic? Is prayer? No, not by definitions 1 and 2.

God: Perfection of Power, Not "Magic"
Definitions 3 and 4 deserve a closer look. If God does miracles, then perhaps the way he does them could fit under definition 3. Certainly, God has supernatural powers (and not just "apparently"!), according to Christian belief.

Here's the problem atheists or skeptics will have with that, however. God's power is (again, according to Christian belief) wrapped up completely in the definition of God. God has power because of who and what He is: the eternal, sovereign (meaning he does what he wills), omniscient, omnipotent one. God's power is an aspect of his perfection, an essential attribute that's necessary to the very being that God is.

So suppose someone removes every connotation of manipulation, control, means, and techniques from "magic." Suppose they exclude humanity from its scope. Suppose they strip away all these connotations and denotations, and they leave nothing left of it but what rightly fits in the Christian conception of God, and then they accuse us of believing in "magic."

I doubt it's psychologically possible actually to do that: to eliminate all these other associations from our minds. But again, let's suppose we could. What would that leave the skeptic with the accusation that we believe God is a supernatural God of perfect sovereignty and power.

I'm comfortable with that. Every believer is comfortable with that. There's nothing to be embarrassed or ashamed of there: it's just true. That's part of what we believe about God.

Misunderstanding, Irrationality, or Deceit?
So if some atheist or skeptic wants to call God "magic," and if by that they mean something like God's perfection of power, I could live with that. It's fine: except for one very important thing. The purpose for using the word is to create cognitive discomfort, which is accomplished only by relying on associations attached to "magic" that belong neither to God, nor to prayer, nor or to miracles.

Thus it's either an act of misunderstanding, illogic, or deceit on the atheist's/skeptic's part.

The Moral of the Story
But look at how effective it can be, in just four words: "Christians believe in magic." It makes us look stupid, superstitious, unthinking. Contrast that with how long my answer here has run. It took a long time to get to this point!

Note, however, that "Christians believe in magic" trades on shadowy, vague, and emotionally-laden associations we have with the

173

word "magic." Notice also that what I've been doing in this blog post has been thinking it through carefully, one step at a time.

There's a moral there: *Thinking is harder than sloganeering.*

There are other lessons to be learned as well: *Sloganeering can be more persuasive than careful thinking.* If you draw forth people's emotions you're likely to have an impact, regardless of what's rational.

September 9, 2013

Seven Steps Toward Clarifying Atheist Vocabulary

"Magic" isn't the only word atheists like to throw at Christians to make us squirm. They'll tell us we believe in an "invisible friend." Or they'll say we're irrational, intolerant, and so on. I say they're using those words very carelessly.

People who stand oppose Christianity often have their own vocabulary for us Christians and our beliefs. We believe in a "magic invisible friend," they say. They talk about us using God as a crutch, being irrational, and the like.

If we have different meanings in mind, conversations are more likely to lead to confusion than conclusions. Therefore I offer these questions and thoughts, in hopes of clarifying atheist vocabulary.

1. *Magic.* Do you mean illusionists' or wizards' little tricks? Or do you mean the eternal Creator God of the universe involving himself purposefully and lovingly in his creation? If the latter, is "magic" really an appropriate label?

2. *Invisible friend.* Do you mean an imaginary boy, girl, or adult that we can "play with" as if he or she were a real human friend? Or do you mean the all-powerful, sovereign, loving, self-sacrificing, omniscient, omnipresent, majestic, and partially hidden God of the universe? If the latter, is "invisible friend" really an appropriate label?

3. *Crutch.* Do you mean something by which people hobble along when they've been injured due to their own inherent frailty — a weakness that you're too good to be subject to yourself? Or do you mean something that enables people to rise up and be more and do more than they could otherwise? (I

speak as one who has had chronic injuries due to a congenital foot condition. I know what crutches are good for.)

4. *Irrational.* Do you define "rational," as most published New Atheists do (see my edited volume *True Reason: Confronting the Irrationality of the New Atheism*) in terms of agreeing with your conclusion that the world must always be interpreted on strictly empirical terms? Or do you define it in terms of the ability to process thoughts from evidence and premises through to a conclusion with valid reasoning? If the former, aren't you begging the question quite irrationally?

5. *Intolerant.* Do you mean unwilling to agree with relaxed standards of truth and morality? If so, that's certainly us. And why are you so intolerant toward our position?

6. *Arrogant.* Do you mean that we're convinced that we know something that's true for both you and us? If so, that's us, too. But why do you arrogantly propose that you know what's true for both you and us?

7. *Judgmental.* Do you mean we are willing to apply ethical and rational standards to beliefs and actions? If so, we agree that's us. Are you judging us for this?

Now I must add this, since we're not always as virtuous as we ought to be. In some situations, it's likely that atheists and skeptics mean the following:

4a. *Irrational:* Unable to process a thought with valid reasoning, from evidences and premises to conclusions.

5a. *Intolerant:* Ornery, unkind, unwilling to associate with people one disagrees with.

6a. *Arrogant:* Proud, contemptuous, holding an attitude of personal superiority.

7a. *Judgmental:* Condemning, smug, unaware of one's own failings.

Sometimes those are valid descriptions. Sometimes we're really like that. In those cases, the best thing we can say is "We agree, and we see the problem. We apologize and we'll try to live in a more reasonable and loving way."

It's always a good idea to make sure we know what words really mean.

November 3, 2013

Bad Tradeoff: Atheists Rejecting the Bible Due to Old Testament Morality

Here's another complaint atheists make: The Old Testament is so filled with immorality, no one could possibly believe it comes from God. Now, there are lots of great ways to answer that through careful interpretation in context of the times. But that takes some specialized knowledge most of us don't have. In this essay, I seek to show that even if you don't know enough to answer it the way specialists do, you still have an answer anyway.

Basically, it's this: If you don't know all that's going on in the Old Testament law, you do know enough of the whole Bible to trust that God is good. And if you can trust that God is good, it's not hard to believe that the Old Testament questions have good answers somewhere — even if you don't know those answers.

Atheists rejecting the Bible due to Old Testament (OT) morality are making a bad tradeoff. Yet they do it anyway. The other day an atheist online told me he could never follow a Bible with — laws like Exodus 21:7–11:

> When a man sells his daughter as a slave, she shall not go out as the male slaves do. If she does not please her master, who has designated her for himself, then he shall let her be redeemed. He shall have no right to sell her to a foreign people, since he has broken faith with her. If he designates her for his son, he shall deal with her as with a daughter. If he takes another wife to himself, he shall not diminish her food, her clothing, or her marital rights. And if he does not do these three things for her, she shall go out for nothing, without payment of money.

Obviously, we have a moral problem with a man selling his daughter as a slave. What kind of a problem is it, though? I suggest it's one of these, in decreasing order of "problem":

1. The moral problem apparent there just isn't resolvable. There is no answer that could possibly make this a moral thing to do.

2. The problem might be resolvable, but given all that we know and all that we could imagine knowing, it really isn't likely

3. It's not resolvable given what we know right now, but we could at least imagine learning something, someday, that would allow us to make sense of it after all.

4. It's resolvable given what we know.

5. It's already been resolved.

When a skeptic says he can't accept a Bible that contains that instruction, he's saying there's an irresolvable moral problem there. Meanwhile some apologists, notably Paul Copan, have dug into the historical context on problems like these, and said they are either resolved or at least resolvable given what we know.

What's a Non-Specialist to Do?
Now, which of these approaches is more intellectually responsible? Especially considering that we're all laymen here when it comes to Ancient Near East studies, should we go with the apologist's answer? Maybe. It's open for consideration, anyway; it's at least possible the apologist has it right. Can we say the same, then, for the skeptic's answer? I don't think so.

That might look as if I'm playing favorites with apologists, but I'm not. I'm taking the reasonable approach instead.

Suppose a specialist in the field says a problem like this has some reasonable solution. He might be right. We laymen wouldn't be able to assess how good that answer is without doing a whole lot of study on our own. But unless there's some obvious error in

179

what the apologist has said, for all we know, there's at least a chance he's got it right.

Maybe, for example, the word "slave" had a completely different meaning then. Maybe it had something to do with perfectly ordinary marriage customs. It doesn't read that way to us in the 21st century Western world, but why would be surprised at the thought that something written so long ago, in such a foreign culture, might mean something different to us now than it did then?

Putting Too Much Stock in Their Imaginations
Indeed, when skeptics point out their so-called obvious errors in apologists' arguments, usually it's easy to see where they're importing today's language and culture into the text, where it has no right to be.

So, it's very difficult in principle to say there's no chance there could ever be any moral resolution to the question. We could never say that unless we knew enough cultural/historical context to make that conclusion certainty.

But when skeptics reject the whole Bible due to passages like these, typically they're saying that the moral problems they present belong either to group 1 or group 2. They're not resolvable in principle, or maybe not resolvable given all that we know or could imagine knowing.

The Most a Skeptic Should Try to Say
But I'd say that's putting way too much faith in the range of their imaginations. The ancient Near East was more different from our world than you think. Or at least that could be the case, and you have no way of knowing that it isn't.

So the most a skeptic should ever try to say is number 3: That it's not resolvable given what we know. Which leaves the door open to the possibility that new knowledge could lead to a satisfying moral answer. Until then, at best, we really only think we know;

we don't know for sure. Nothing more definite than that can be rationally or reasonably justified.

So with that in mind, let's take another look at the atheist's statement I opened with here: he could never follow a religion that includes instructions like we see here in Exodus 21.

What Do We Actually Know?

My answer would be that it's better to look at what we can know than what we cannot. Based on other study in the Bible, we can know:

- The Bible presents the highest example of moral character in all history: Jesus Christ.

- The world would be a better place to live if people would just follow the Ten Commandments. It would even be better if we treated one another according to just numbers 5 through 10 (1 through 4 are tied more to worship than to interpersonal ethics).

- While there remain some gaps, and not everything in it is corroborated, the Bible's historical record is completely consistent with all the definite external information available through documents and archaeology.

- God revealed himself thoroughly and uniquely as a God of love.

- He expressed that love through the highest possible means, self-sacrifice on the Cross.

The Tradeoff: Good or Bad?

What's apparently bad in the Bible is (admittedly) apparently outrageously bad. What's good in the Bible is certainly, knowably, outrageously, stupendously good.

We can make our decisions based on what we know or what we don't know. Choosing such a great, known good like that is perfectly reasonable. It tells us a great deal about the character of God. If there's any reason to think God is consistent in character — and there is, though I don't have space to go into it here — and if there's also reason to think the same God who was responsible for the Old Testament laws, it's also reasonable to think he had good reasons for those laws. Even if we don't get it.

An atheist who rejects all the outrageous good that we do know, based on some questionable, unknown passage about which we can't know nearly enough, is making a bad tradeoff, rationally, morally, and experientially.

November 30, 2017

Naturalism

Atheists are inordinately fond of naturalism, the view that reality consists in matter and energy interacting in law-like manner, and (except for the few hardy souls who will admit the reality of abstract things like numbers) nothing else. Nothing supernatural, in particular.

It really isn't that solid a worldview after all.

Only Natural

There have been many debates on the Thinking Christian *blog about "philosophical naturalism," the view that nothing exists except matter, energy, and their interactions according to law and chance, and that there is no supernatural. For some people, then, the world we live in is "only natural." Whatever happens, happens because the laws of physics make it happen. It ends up looking pretty much like machines, everywhere you look.*

This short story, my only work of fiction in this book, is intended as a commentary on that view. Some characters are of course borrowed from The Wonderful Wizard of Oz *by L. Frank Baum, written in 1900, now in the public domain.*

Did you know there were two tin woodmen in Oz? Probably not — the second one speaks for the first time in this short snippet of a story. What happens in an "only natural" world?

Only Natural

"He thought it was a curse. I saw it differently. You probably remember his story — how he fell in love with a certain girl, who happened to be my niece. Her mother, my poor late brother's widow, didn't want her girl getting married, so she went to the witch to buy a hex on the fellow. Next time he went out to the woods, his axe slipped and cut a horrible gash in his leg.

"There was nothing to be done for it, the leg was lost; so he went to the tinsmith and got a replacement. He had no idea his axe had been turned against him, so he went right back to chopping. Next time he went to the woods, he lost one arm to it, then another — and then in the end he was all tin.

"I didn't understand what was going on any more than he did. Anyone could have known *something* was up, though. He wasn't

185

that bad at handling an axe! Somehow he was oblivious to what was really going on, though, and he kept right on cutting wood, and cutting himself.

"Maybe there was a spell on him, too — I can't believe it was just his axe that was addled. You'd think he'd have thought it was pretty remarkable to survive with a tin body, but he took it in stride — as long as he was well oiled, that is. His one big complaint was he had lost his heart.

"Well, I'm a woodman too. I saw what he never saw. Oh, he was happy enough over his new tin body, all shiny and all, and he was glad to have a skin that the axe couldn't cut any more. But he was so caught up in not having a heart, he never figured out just how much good the spell had done him. He was a woodcutting machine! Fast, accurate, never bothered by brambles or nettles; why, he could keep going and going with hardly a break except to oil up.

"And he had the gall to complain about it!

"He didn't know — not until it was way too late — just who it was who had caused this. But I knew. His old girlfriend's mother was having one of those little gossip sessions with my wife, complaining about this and that. I overheard enough to figure out how it all came down.

"My wife, now — bless her — she was one of my own bigger mistakes. She would get into these gripe-fests with other women, never complained about anything but one thing: me. 'He's lazy, he doesn't make us any money, he treats me rotten,' and on and on.

"I couldn't stand it. What did she know about woodcutting? I swung that axe all day long, sweating, blistering my hands, never knowing when some idiot with another axe was going to drop a tree on my head — and all she could do was whine.

186

"Okay, I'll admit she wasn't all wrong. Woodcutting is a hard life. We never had any money to spare, hardly enough food to eat, and our home was just about falling apart. That's how it was until I got things figured out.

"It was lucky, in a way, how I happened to overhear them talking. (Usually I stay as far away as I can.) My sister-in-law was crowing to about how she had gone to the Wicked Witch of the East, and how it had cost her just two sheep and a cow to get this spell cast.

"Which gave me the idea. It was only natural, don't you think? We didn't have any livestock to spare at the time, but I figured I could make a deal to pay the witch later, once I got myself improved.

"The witch went for it: the same deal she asked from my sister-in-law. Now, you're probably thinking she would have had some huge evil trick in mind; but no, she may be a wicked witch, but she kept her word. A few good chops and a visit to the tinsmith, that's all it took; then two sheep and a cow, as soon as I could afford them. Hey, I did okay; that's all she got out of me.

"I really don't need animals like that now anyway — tin men don't eat, and we don't mind about keeping warm. I just have to keep my joints oiled up. I may not have a heart, but then, I wasn't all that lovey-dovey with my wife anyway, if you know what I mean.

"I hardly ever think about a tree falling on me anymore; the other woodcutters mostly stay clear of my part of the woods. I move a lot faster now.

"Why *do* they call her a wicked witch, anyway?"

July 18, 2006

Says the Madman: Humanity is Dead, and We Are Its Murderers

There's a very famous passage on "the death of God" in the writings of Friedrich Nietzsche. In it he has a "Madman" crying out, "Whither is God? ... I will tell you. We have killed him — you and I. All of us are his murderers."[13]

The passage goes on to speak of how horrible it is that God has been "murdered." Of course, God had no difficulty surviving this so-called death. Now, though, there's a real sense in which atheism is killing humanity. Here in this essay I borrow from Nietzsche to show the horror of that more contemporary "murder." It's not "Whither is God? We have killed him." It's "Whither is humanity? We have killed it."

"'Whither is humanity?' cried the Madman. 'I will tell you. We have killed it. We are its murderers! But how could we do this? Are we not plunging continually? How shall we comfort ourselves, the murderers of all murderers?'"

When Friedrich Nietzsche's Madman told the world, *"God is dead, and we are his murderers,"* it was as if he alone understood the enormity of the crime. This deicide was never anything but a fiction: Nietzsche never thought there was a real God who could really be killed, rather he saw *the idea of God* dying in the European mind. (Others knew God was alive, laughing at the Madman.)

The "Death of God"
It took a Nietzsche to fathom the depths of what this "death of God" would mean:

---

13   http://www.historyguide.org/europe/madman.html

How could we drink up the sea? Who gave us the sponge to wipe away the entire horizon? What were we doing when we unchained this earth from its sun? Whither is it moving now? Whither are we moving? Away from all suns? Are we not plunging continually? Backward, sideward, forward, in all directions? Is there still any up or down? Are we not straying, as through an infinite nothing? Do we not feel the breath of empty space? Has it not become colder? Is not night continually closing in on us? Do we not need to light lanterns in the morning? Do we hear nothing as yet of the noise of the gravediggers who are burying God? Do we smell nothing as yet of the divine decomposition? Gods, too, decompose. God is dead. God remains dead. And we have killed him...."

Here the madman fell silent and looked again at his listeners; and they, too, were silent and stared at him in astonishment. At last he threw his lantern on the ground, and it broke into pieces and went out. "I have come too early," he said then; "my time is not yet. This tremendous event is still on its way, still wandering; it has not yet reached the ears of men. Lightning and thunder require time; the light of the stars requires time; deeds, though done, still require time to be seen and heard. This deed is still more distant from them than most distant stars — and yet they have done it themselves."

The Death of Humanity
And what if the Madman were to survey the world today? Would he not would cry out, "Humanity is dead!" Yes! And he would ask, "Do we hear nothing as yet of the noise of the gravediggers who are burying humanity? Do we smell nothing as yet of the human decomposition?" And he might again conclude that his time is not yet.

How have we killed humanity? you ask. *Is this not more clearly a fiction than Nietzsche's "God is dead" ever was? Are there not 7 billion persons who can witness to humanity's vitality?*

189

Yes, humanity still lives, just as God still lived in Nietzsche's day. Humanity lives in spite of the universal mass murder that philosophical naturalism would inflict upon it: the attempted strangulation of the very *idea* of the human. Its quest is the murder not of persons but of personhood, not of humans but of humanness itself.

Naturalism will not succeed in this. *That does not mean it is not trying.*

I do not lay this charge directly at the naturalist's feet: it is *naturalism* that is culpable, not those who are naturalists. Instead I call you to account, you who are naturalists, for your blithe and foolish ignorance of the magnitude of the atrocities you endorse. You bring carnage, and you speak of it lovingly, as if it brings hope to your breast. Who gave you the sponge to wipe away your concern for the heart of humanness?

The Deathly Doctrine of Naturalism

Here is the deathliness of your naturalism:

Your naturalism seeks to kill humanness — and thus *all the dignity of humanity* — when it tells us we're machines, lacking all freedom of will.

It seeks to kill humanness — and thus *all the realized experience of humanity* — when it tries to persuade us human consciousness is but an illusion.

It seeks to kill humanity — *all the glory of being human* — when it places us on a plane with the animals and charges us with "speciesism" for considering ourselves otherwise.

It seeks to kill humanity — *all the integral wholeness of the human* — when it claims we are but machines crafted and co-opted by genes to reproduce themselves.

It seeks to kill humanity — *all of humanity, all of humanness* — when it tells us that physics and chemistry provide the most real, the truest explanation for who and what we are.

And all of this is to say nothing of the death of humanity in relation to the living God, who imparted humanity to us as beings in his own image.

Be Not Blind to This Death

Naturalism's success would mean the destruction of all humanness everywhere. The universal murder would be accomplished. The genocide would be complete.

This is preposterous! you say. *Where is this death of which you speak?*

Do you not see it, though it is right before your eyes? ("I have come too early," said the Madman; "my time is not yet.")

And again you say, *Call me not a murderer! I too am human. I will not kill; I will not accept such a charge upon me!*

Yes, naturalist, you are human. It is your humanness that may save you in the end.

You say consciousness is an illusion, yet you say so *consciously.* You *choose* to say that choice is impossible. Your doctrine of fragmented reductionism issues not from your genes and neurotransmitters but from yourself: a person; a real person; a whole person.

Your abstract naturalism unleashes its philosophical weapons of mass destruction upon humanness everywhere; still, your own very real humanness survives. So while you claim the murderous doctrine with your words, with your life you deny it; and how good it is that you do, for that very denial means your survival as a human person.

So Great a Horror

Nietzsche gloried in the horror of God's "death." Would he regard humanity's death the same way? I can hardly think he would, even though today's deadly naturalism is a tree nourished in the earth piled on God's fictional grave. Nietzsche proclaimed God's death as the liberation of humanity, but there finally comes a point when no so great a horror can no longer hide under such a mask.

For though naturalism is an abstraction, its weapons have real effects that inflict real damage, just as the fiction of God's death has had real effects.

The more the naturalist insists that we are but meat computers, puppets of our chemistry and environment, laboring under an illusion of human glory, meaning, and uniqueness, when we ought to reject our speciesism and bow to the knowledge of our bland sameness — the more the naturalist and the rest of us believe such things, and the more we will act as if they were real. We will treat ourselves and each other according to the degraded view we assign ourselves and others.

Has it not happened already in the wasteland of the TV sitcom? You say that is a trivial example. Is that not the point? We have trivialized our days and our evenings. We have trivialized our economic lives: our highest goal is not to serve but to survive until one day we can walk out of our work with the right gadgets, onto the right golf course. We have degraded romance and intimacy into the virtually anonymous "hook-up." We have degraded marriage into a come-and-go-as-you-please convenience. We have trivialized all our human experience: because we have taught ourselves humanness itself is trivial.

Weapons Strapped Upon Themselves

Therefore to the naturalist I say this: you have strapped your deadly weapons upon your own body, for there is no escape, no exception: this is your suicide, by which you also murder all humanity. Would you die for this? Would you deny your entire humanness for this?

Nietzsche's Madman understood better than others (though not well enough) what the God-killers were clamoring to destroy. He would know today (though not well enough) what it means that so many seek to strangle all humanness out of all human beings.

God survived the Madman. The Madman is, in the end, quite mad. Humanity will survive his re-visitation.

Postscript: For Those Who May Care

It bears repeating: Naturalism has grown up out of the fictional grave of God. Ironically some naturalists call themselves "humanists." I speak again to you who consider yourself a naturalist: perhaps you do not care about God. Maybe you find the thought of God loathsome to you. I do not know what might have led you there. I would dearly love to call you to the place where you could understand that God is really good, loving, and great; to help you see that whatever you find ugly in God is founded in some distortion or misconception, rather than in reality.

If you could answer that call, I would be happy to greet you in the company of those who, by God's grace, have come to experience his truth and goodness.

That may be too long and difficult a step for you to take. It might involve a change of mind that for you at this stage is beyond even imagining. Then I ask you to consider taking a smaller step in the right direction. I ask you to consider a step toward affirming your own humanness, and that of all the people you know and love. Give up telling yourself with words what your real self knows to be false. Affirm — do not deny as "illusion" — your own freedom, your own awareness, your own worth beyond that of the animals. You are human, and you know it.

The genocide of which I have been speaking here is abstract, not real. In the end our humanness will prevail after all. Let your own humanness prevail in you — even if it leads you one frightening step toward God.

January 24, 2012

Christians and Atheists: Sharing One Planet, Living in Two Worlds

Blogging has a way of bringing people together who never would have met otherwise. Here, it is Christians and atheists. We don't tend to run in the same circles in our social lives, and we don't often talk about these kinds of issues at work, so this is unique in many ways.

It's very stimulating, and it's given me new perspective on the so-called "culture wars." I wonder whether we've chosen the wrong metaphor. It's not so much a war between cultures as it is two worlds, vastly different from one another, coexisting on the same planet.

There is a world of those who believe in God as creator of the universe and all life; the sovereign, merciful ruler; the source of all goodness and beauty; the ground of all truth, including moral truth; the One revealed in Scripture and made manifest through Jesus Christ, who lived, died and rose again; the One on whom we depend for rescue from death due to our own rebellion from him; the one who gives life to those who accept it.

For atheists and secularists, none of this is real. None of it. I wrote in the previous chapter about our differences. They're huge. The Bible is certainly realistic about this. Jesus said, "If the world hates you, you know that it hated me before it hated you" (from John 15:18–25). This was not paranoia speaking: Jesus himself stood against the order of the day and was killed for it.

Two Worlds, Continued...
Those who follow Jesus still stand against the familiar world order, often called simply "the world" in the New Testament.

- The world says to get ahead; Jesus said, "If anyone desires to be first, he shall be last and servant of all."

- The world says to get what you can get; Jesus said, "It is more blessed to give than to receive."

- The world says to get even; Jesus said, "For if you forgive men their trespasses [sins, offenses], your heavenly Father will also forgive you. But if you do not forgive men their trespasses, neither will your Father forgive your trespasses."

- The world says to hold on for dear life; Jesus said, "For whoever desires to save his life will lose it, but whoever loses his life for My sake will find it."

- The world says to run your own life; Jesus said, speaking of himself, "For even the Son of Man did not come to be served, but to serve, and to give His life a ransom for many."

- The world says to figure things out for we; Jesus said to rely on the Scriptures as the very seed of life.

- The world says we are self-sufficient; Jesus said, "Unless you are converted and become as little children, you will by no means enter the kingdom of heaven."

- The world says all paths lead to the same end; Jesus said, "I am the way, the truth, and the life. No one comes to the Father except through Me."

So here we see two systems, diametrically opposed to each other in their most fundamental values. And why is that? In the passage above where Jesus speaks of being hated by the world, it is because in him the sin of the world stands exposed.

Standing at a Distance

Col. 1:13 says believers have been transferred from the domain of darkness into the kingdom of God's beloved Son. That's what's going on. Two kingdoms, two worlds. Is it any wonder that Christians have trouble finding common ground with atheists?

We stand at such a distance from each other. For many unbelievers, considering the possibility of a supernatural and sovereign creator is strange, maybe even repulsive. For me, on the other hand, the thought of a cosmos barren of such a loving creative source seems horribly wrong. And it runs counter to what I know and have long experienced to be true.

The God I have known in this way is deeply wonderful and satisfying. I can only pray and hope that some unbeliever will be motivated to explore his reality.

Which World Is the Real World?
This leads to two great questions. The first is, which (if either) of these worlds has it right? The test is which one makes the most sense as a complete system. If I am right — and I'm betting my life on it — then the Biblical viewpoint stands the test of being consistent with its own teachings and with what we know to be true of life and of ourselves.

Meeting One Another In Our Humanness
The second great question is, where shall we go to meet one another, we denizens of such different worlds? I suggest it is in our humanness; for we share more than a world, we share a common human condition.

We know what it is to face our joys and our pains. We know particularly what it's like to be misunderstood, misrepresented, stereotyped. We know what it's like not to be listened to.

This, by the way, is one reason I focus a lot of my writing on our essential humanness: If we lose our common grip on that, then I don't know what could bring us together. We live in two worlds, but we have to find a place to meet on common ground.

February 28, 2014. Adapted from a blog post previously published October 7, 2005, at https://www.thinkingchristian.net/wp-content/uploads/2014/02/index.html.

Getting "Faith" Wrong — and Right

When atheist activist Peter Boghossian wrote *A Manual for Creating Atheists,* he defined faith in all kinds of false and tendentious ways — and created a delivery vehicle for spreading the error. I responded with the book *Peter Boghossian: Atheist Tactician,* and with a lot of blog activity besides. Here's some that you might not see from other sources.

No, Atheists and Skeptics: Christian Faith is Not a Failed Epistemology

I keep hearing from atheists and skeptics that "faith is a failed epistemology." (Epistemology is the philosophical study of how we can know what we know or think we know.) What these people mean is that if religion is something we know by faith, then we don't know it at all, because there are too many ways to go wrong in "knowing by faith."

Now, if faith were indeed a way of knowing, in the sense that they're talking about, they would be right. It's a completely unreliable way to "know." There's no objective check on what we "know" that way.

And that may be the way some religions work. I think Mormonism is probably an example. It's not true of Christianity, though.

This is another one of my more technical essays in this book. The next one covers similar ground but uses more familiar biblical language.

Skeptics say Christianity is disconnected from reality — especially the "faith" part of it, by which we come to believe what we believe. "Faith" is just a bad way to know things. We need facts instead. But the skeptics are wrong from the start.

In Christianity there is knowledge and then there is faith. I am not speaking of the order of salvation here — the sequence of events in our minds, hearts, and souls by which God reveals himself personally to the one who is being saved. God grants faith as a gift (Eph. 2:8–9) which opens the eyes (2 Cor. 4:3–6, 1 Cor. 2:14–15) to enable his people to apprehend truths to which we would otherwise be blind.

Faith Rests on Knowledge

That's one way of looking at the faith-knowledge sequence. It's a description of God's initiative in persons' hearts. But there is another logical sequence that better describes the relation between faith and knowledge. It's illustrated well in what Paul said in 2 Corinthians 4:13–14:

> Since we have the same spirit of faith according to what has been written, "I believed, and so I spoke," we also believe, and so we also speak, knowing that he who raised the Lord Jesus will raise us also with Jesus and bring us with you into his presence.

The quotation is from Psalm 116:10 (actually Psalm 115:1 in the Septuagint version). The logical sequence here is different from the order in which Paul wrote it, so let's clarify it this way:

1. Paul knows that God raised Jesus from the dead.

10. Not written but in the background: Paul knows that Jesus promised resurrection to his followers (John 14:1–8).

11. Thus he believes that God will raise him and others from the dead.

12. Because he believes, he speaks.

First there is knowledge. The Tyndale commentary on this passage says, "Paul's faith is strengthened by the knowledge that the God who raised Jesus from the dead will also raise him along with Jesus." Paul's knowledge doesn't follow his faith, rather his faith follows his knowledge.

Faith Is Trusting in What One Knows

The step Paul takes in number 3 is a step of faith. There's no demonstrable proof that he or his readers will be raised from the dead. His confidence in his future resurrection is based in his trust in Jesus' promise and in his knowledge that Jesus himself was raised. Thus faith for Paul (and for all biblical Christianity) is a matter of trusting in what one knows. That trust is well placed,

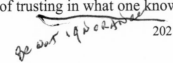

given the reality of what Paul knew. It's a leap, sure, but it's a sensible one in view of the known facts; a leap from light into light, not a leap into the dark.

It's a Rational Response

Now it does almost appear that we know certain things by faith. How does Paul know he'll be resurrected? By connecting the dots between Jesus' resurrection and his promises, and trusting that the promise will be fulfilled. He might put it this way:

a. I know Jesus was resurrected.

b. I know because of Jesus' own resurrection that there is power in God to raise me from the dead.

c. I know Jesus promised me resurrection if I follow him.

d. I know Jesus' character has been shown trustworthy in every observable way.

e. I know enough, therefore, to put high confidence in his promise. My confidence is high enough to call it knowledge.

The jump from (d) to (e) might look like a faith leap — but it isn't. It's a rational inference. If (a) through (d) are true, then it's rational to draw the conclusion (e).

Where then does faith enter in? It's in (f):

f. Therefore I will choose to trust the One who has been demonstrated trustworthy.

That's not a way of knowing; rather, once again, it's an attitude toward what one knows. opens faith channel to grace

Why So Much Confusion Over This?

More specifically, faith is an attitude of relational trust. I've had skeptics tell me that's not so. They're simply wrong on that.

annos — on surgery table.

Ju gov board

It's *trust,* in the Greek, it's *trust,* in every biblical usage (sometimes with more emphasis on relationship). It's *trust,* in the lexicons and the dictionaries. It's *trust,* in every credibly written theology. Biblical, Christian faith has always been *relational trust.*

Why then do atheists and skeptics say it's a failed epistemology, or that it's "believing what we know isn't true," or "pretending to know what we can't know"? I can think of two possible reasons.

Christian Confusion and "Christian" Confusion

First, some are uninformed or maybe confused. Some Christians are partly to blame for that, since not all believers have thought carefully about the relation between faith and knowledge. That's to be expected, by the way: not all Christians even care about that relation; they can live out their faith happily enough without thinking about it. (I think they could grow stronger in faith if they thought about it more, but I would never say their faith is unreal just because they can't articulate it this way.)

So they'll tell people their faith is "how I know God is real," or some such thing. They just don't know how to explain it better than that. That doesn't mean that's the best or most accurate way to explain it. We don't derive definitions and explanations from people who haven't thought much about it.

It's also the case that some people claiming the "Christian" name, having given it some thought, actually believe faith is "how we know." This is confusing indeed. My response would be that they've got a mistaken view of Christ and the Bible in history. I would place them in the same category as the other religions I mentioned in the third paragraph of this article.

Or, Why So Much Misdirection?

The other reason skeptics and atheists describe faith so wrongly is because they want to make it look bad. It's a self-serving move on their part. I'm convinced this is the case for the more prominent atheist writers on "faith," including Dawkins, Coyne, Harris, and

204

Boghossian. They've found a way to make faith stupid by definition. They hammer on that definition, hoping to persuade people
by mere loud repetition that their view on it carries more authority
than Christians' view — even though Christians are the ones with
the intellectual heritage and experience to know.

They try to paint Christianity as stupid and anti-intellectual. They
have to ignore all the relevant literature on the subject to do so.
Who's being anti-intellectual?

Eyes That Need Opening
But then there is the blindness of which I spoke earlier. The reality is indisputable: thoughtful informed Christians have *never*
treated faith or thought of it in the way many atheists want to define it. But they treat it as if their definitions were the only correct
ones; the only accurate way to describe faith. (Boghossian says so
explicitly.)

In other words, their definition of faith is wrong — — obviously
wrong. Yet still they press their case, confident as if they had
every reason for it. Why won't they open their eyes?

Faith Is a Reasonable Response to What We Know
Faith is not a way of knowing, but an attitude of confidence regarding what one knows. Often it's confidence in spite of what
one sees; for one can know what one cannot currently see. It's
been described as remaining confident in the dark of what one has
seen in the light. Christian faith is not a failed epistemology, it's a
reasonable attitude in response to what we can know to be true.

December 19, 2016

Two Views of Faith

In the previous essay I wrote about the relation between faith and knowledge. I take up the same topic here, though from a much more familiar biblical angle. Did the disciples actually know anything about Jesus when they decided to follow him? Or did they make their decisions based on some fact-free "faith"?

Some time ago a commenter on *Thinking Christian* wrote, "The core problem is that religion teaches that holding absolute beliefs without evidence (*aka* faith) is a virtue."

Is that what faith is? No, actually not. The other day in a Bible study at church, I noticed a great way to illustrate the difference between this and true faith. It's in the intersection of the gospels.

None of the gospels tells every detail of Jesus' life, and no two gospels cover the same details. In this case, looking at just part of the story makes it look like faith is something like a flash out of the blue; looking at the rest of it shows that faith is based on solid information.

The account I'm talking about is Jesus' calling Peter to be one of his followers. All four gospels cover this event. Two of the accounts are very similar, and it is very likely that Matthew borrowed from Mark here:

Matthew 4:18–20 (all scriptures quoted from the ESV):

> While walking by the Sea of Galilee, he saw two brothers, Simon (who is called Peter) and Andrew his brother, casting a net into the sea, for they were fishermen. And he said to them, "Follow me, and I will make you fishers of men." Immediately they left their nets and followed him.

Mark 1:16–18:

> Passing alongside the Sea of Galilee, he saw Simon and An-
> drew the brother of Simon casting a net into the sea, for they
> were fishermen. And Jesus said to them, "Follow me, and I
> will make you become fishers of men." And immediately
> they left their nets and followed him.

Not a Mere Leap

This looks a lot like the way some people conceive of faith. You
meet someone or get some kind of idea or impression, and boom!
you change everything you think about the world. There's no evidence, no logic, no background, no thinking.

Now, I do not mean to distort the purpose or message of these
two accounts. If they do not teach a clear message about how
faith is acquired, that is because that was not their authors' intent.
I mean this instead as an illustration of how faith can be misunderstood by those who think they have the full context, when in
fact they do not. Let's broaden our view to get a more complete
picture, starting with the Gospel of John.

John 1:35–42:

> The next day again John [the Baptist] was standing with two
> of his disciples, and he looked at Jesus as he walked by and
> said, "Behold, the Lamb of God!" The two disciples heard
> him say this, and they followed Jesus. Jesus turned and saw
> them following and said to them, "What are you seeking?"
> And they said to him, "Rabbi" (which means Teacher),
> "where are you staying?" He said to them, "Come and you
> will see." So they came and saw where he was staying, and
> they stayed with him that day, for it was about the tenth hour.
> One of the two who heard John speak and followed Jesus was
> Andrew, Simon Peter's brother. He first found his own
> brother Simon and said to him, "We have found the Messiah"
> (which means Christ). He brought him to Jesus. Jesus looked

at him and said, "So you are Simon the son of John? You shall be called Cephas" (which means Peter).

Here we discover that Peter's brother had been a disciple of John the Baptist, and we know that John had been preaching about Jesus Christ. So Peter had much more than just a glance from Jesus to go on, he had very strong personal references!

Knowledge Feeds Faith

Interestingly, some scholars think this event may have taken place a full year before Jesus came and called Peter, as recorded in the passages quoted above. Jesus seems to have had a one-year period of ministry in Judea (where Jerusalem is) early in his time of ministry. This event with Andrew was probably before that year, and the final call to Peter was probably afterward, when Jesus traveled the 70 or so miles north to begin his Galilean ministry. If that's true, then Peter had plenty of time to think about this great man he had met, to ponder his teachings, and to hear of his reputation.

Still, though, even if that's not the case, the additional picture we have in Luke tells us *even more clearly* what Peter was working from when he decided to follow Christ. He had seen Christ at work (Luke 4:38–39):

And he [Jesus] arose and left the synagogue and entered Simon's house. Now Simon's mother-in-law was ill with a high fever, and they appealed to him on her behalf. And he stood over her and rebuked the fever, and it left her, and immediately she rose and began to serve them.

Plus even more (Luke 5:1–11):

On one occasion, while the crowd was pressing in on him to hear the word of God, he was standing by the lake of Gennesaret, and he saw two boats by the lake, but the fishermen had gone out of them and were washing their nets. Getting into one of the boats, which was Simon's, he asked him to put out a little from the land. And he sat down and taught the people from the boat.

And when he had finished speaking, he said to Simon, "Put out into the deep and let down your nets for a catch." And Simon answered, "Master, we toiled all night and took nothing! But at your word I will let down the nets." And when they had done this, they enclosed a large number of fish, and their nets were breaking. They signaled to their partners in the other boat to come and help them. And they came and filled both the boats, so that they began to sink.

But when Simon Peter saw it, he fell down at Jesus' knees, saying, "Depart from me, for I am a sinful man, O Lord." For he and all who were with him were astonished at the catch of fish that they had taken, and so also were James and John, sons of Zebedee, who were partners with Simon. And Jesus said to Simon, "Do not be afraid; from now on you will be catching men." And when they had brought their boats to land, they left everything and followed him.

Peter never "left everything and followed him" until after he had possibly had a year to think through what he knew at first about Jesus. He had certainly seen Jesus heal his wife's mother, heard Jesus teach at least once, and seen Jesus perform the miracle of the fish.

So Peter's faith in following Jesus was no blind leap. It was based on an experienced reality, real information he had real opportunity to reflect upon. He might have asked himself still,

Of course he still had to have faith to follow. He was trusting his whole life and future to this teacher Jesus, and to the God whom Jesus taught. But it was not belief against the evidence. It was belief based on evidences and experience.

March 31, 2009

No Evidence for Faith

Atheists — especially the more strident "New Atheists" following Richard Dawkins's lead — like to say there's no evidence for faith. Surprisingly, they're right in a way. But it's because they're using the word when they talk about "faith" that way. Faith isn't what they think it is. I use their words against them in a way, in this essay, to show that evidence, faith, and knowledge really do go together; just not the way they think it should.

The New Atheists are right: there's no evidence for faith!

Surprised? Here's the answer: They're only right based on a complete misunderstanding of faith, and how faith relates to evidence-based factual knowledge and rational inference. At the end of the day, there is evidence for faith after all.

Confused? Read on. It will become clear.

The New Atheist Charge: No Evidence for Faith

The typical New Atheist position is that there's no evidence for faith, by definition; for if there was evidence it would produce knowledge, not faith. This is a standard line of argument among their camp.

It would be nice if they gave it at least the respect of saying there is *insufficient* evidence, rather than *no* evidence. But that's impossible if one believes the premise *if there was evidence, it would lead to knowledge, not faith.*

But wait: there really is no evidence for faith!

Christians do present evidence, despite opinions to the contrary. Just what is it, though, that we're presenting evidence for? Is it really faith? I say no: we do not present evidence for faith.

And with that, I've given up the game, right? No. Stick with me a moment and I'll explain why that's wrong.

Evidence for Facts and Inferences Instead

Let's look a moment at what Christian apologists like myself typically seek to demonstrate through the use of evidence. This is but a small sampling of our work, but it will serve a very important purpose.

- We use *philosophical arguments* to show that there is a reasonably high probability that God exists. These are based on evidence such as:

  - The non-eternality of the physical universe

  - The unique nature of humans, including rationality, consciousness, moral responsibility, and so on.

  - The fine-tuning of the universe to permit chemical complexity, and thereby life itself

  - The existential conflict of humans: our awareness of falling short of something better

  - etc.

- We use *textual studies* to show that we have trustworthy versions of the original biblical documents.

- We use *historical studies* to show that there is considerable demonstrable truth in the Gospels.

- We use *biblical studies* to demonstrate the remarkable consistency the Bible demonstrates from beginning to end, on both the thematic and the detail level.

- We use *historical studies,* again, to show that there are facts for which the Resurrection of Jesus Christ is the best-fitting explanation, provided that it's not examined from an anti-supernaturalist perspective.

- We use *philosophical metaphysics* and the *philosophy of history* to show that there is no good reason to assume an *a priori*

211

anti-supernaturalist stance in examining the Resurrection narrative.

- We use *philosophical arguments* to show that ontological naturalism (a prominent form of atheism) is unlikely to be true.

And so on.

Whether these sorts of evidence are *sufficient* is a question for another day. For now the question is, *for what are they evidence?* Do any of them work as evidence *for faith?* Not exactly. See the list again. These types of evidence (coupled with arguments) count toward the existence of God, the trustworthiness of our contemporary Bible, the truth of the Gospel narratives, the likelihood that Jesus Christ actually rose from the dead, and the unlikelihood that naturalism is true.

In other words, they lead to conclusions about the nature of reality, and about events in history. *They're not evidence for faith — not directly, that is, although indirectly they certainly are.*

Where then does faith come in? I have two answers to offer.

Evidence for *The Faith,* and Evidence for the Rational Inferences That Support Faith

First, there is "the faith," that is, the body of beliefs that make up Christian doctrine. Then there is personal faith, which is an individual's belief and/or trust in the implications of what we know to be true.

For example, given that there are good reasons to believe:

- The Bible is reliable as history

- The Resurrection of Jesus Christ really happened, and

- God is revealed in multiple ways as a promise-making and promise-keeping God,

I conclude that I can trust him with my eternal condition.

Many Christians have taken that trust all the way to giving up their lives on earth in faithful expectation of a good outcome after death. That's a Christian expression of faith.

Faith Follows the Rational Inference

It really is a step of faith, still, for we cannot see the future into which God is leading us. We live in a confusing and often contrary world, and we ourselves are confusing and contrary individuals. C. S. Lewis rightly said that faith is continuing to believe what we know is true even when our emotions tell us it isn't. It's a matter of holding on to the truth we've recognized in the light, even when the world turns dark on us. It's remaining faith-*full* toward what we know, and *faithful* to the God we're coming to know.

We could contrast Christian faith with a very similar Muslim expression of faith; for many Islamists have thought they would gain a better eternity by sacrificing their lives in *jihad*. What makes our faith any different from theirs? Why would I be confident in my faith and not theirs? It's because of the evidential basis for the facts on which my faith rests. When we say we have evidence for faith, that's what we mean: we have evidence for the facts upon which we rest our faith.

Why the New Atheists Are Wrong About Faith Being a Way of Knowing

So now we can circle back around to the atheists' error of setting up faith as a way of knowing and then knocking it down. We have seen that for Christians, faith is typically an attitude toward what is known, not a way of knowing.

Specifically, it's an attitude of trust in the implications of what is known. Evidence and reasoning take us as far as the conclusion (using the same example as before) that we can trust God with our eternal lives. Faith is the actual placing of trust in what evidence and reasoning have shown us to be true.

Peter Boghossian, author of *A Manual for Creating Atheists,* and others say faith is an unreliable way of knowing. Their biggest error is not in the word "unreliable." It's in considering faith to be primarily a way of knowing. It could hardly be an unreliable way of knowing unless it were a way of knowing in the first place.

There Really Is Evidence for Faith After All
It's still okay if someone speaks of "evidence for faith." It's a useful shorthand. Just remember that it's short for, "evidence for the facts upon which we rest our faith." Then you won't make the atheists' mistake.

January 29, 2014

Part 6: Social and Ethical Challenges

I mentioned this already in the introduction to the book, but it bears repeating: Christianity's most important "fault" these days isn't that it's "false," it's that it's "bad," "intolerant," "exclusive," and above all, "homophobic."

Of course we can do bad things. If I had to look back to the last time I was mistreated by a Christian, I'd only half to reach back in time to this morning. Which is also the last time I did the same myself. Even though it was in an interaction where we everyone present was seeking to be honorable and Christ-honoring, our humanness came out. I know that happens to you as well.

The answer to the charge of Christian badness comes on many levels. One, of course, is to live more in line with Christ's character., recognizing along the way that we'll never get close enough to represent him as he really deserves, but pursuing his holiness anyway with all the grace he gives us.

But we could live perfectly, and it wouldn't satisfy everyone. Jesus proved that himself. One reason is because of mixed-up views on what it means to live a good and decent life. Is it through "tolerance"? That's the word these days, but in fact tolerance isn't all it's cracked up to be. I have three articles on that in this section.

Or do we live the good life by promoting new views on sexuality? No, not that, either, as I explain in three more articles.

And finally, I close the book with three less closely-connected articles on moral improvement, and religious freedom in America.

Tolerance is Too Weak

Tolerance has become America's supreme virtue. In a pluralistic society, where values clash and cultures collide, it's the new glue that's supposed to hold us all together. It's also the philosophy underlying "political correctness," and the plea of almost all groups who feel misunderstood.

Unfortunately, it won't work.

Tolerance is a "virtue" that could never work. Why? Because at its core, it's a weak idea. It may start off in the right direction, but it doesn't go nearly far enough. Where it stops is wholly inadequate.

Webster defines tolerance as "the act of allowing something; sympathy or indulgence of practices differing or conflicting with one's own. In practice these days, it usually means leaving one another alone, letting others do and be as they wish without interference. Therein lies its weakness.

For in letting others alone, and not interfering, we separate ourselves from one another. We become divided into our groups. We sanction differences without understanding them. Tolerance breaks down none of the walls between people; it merely tells us to accept the walls and live with them, maybe even try to pretend they aren't there.

A More Noble Set of Virtues

So why not choose stronger words: *respect* and *love* instead of *tolerance?* Respect implies understanding and appreciation. How much better if I respect another culture than if I merely tolerate it! This brings people together.

Love unites us still further, even in our differences: Jesus taught us to love even our enemies. This causes us to come into contact, to break down walls. We can acknowledge differences without separating people.

In the full Christian understanding of the word, *love* can even allow us to have a good disagreement. I have had a couple of friends who are gay men; one has died of AIDS. In that whole time of tragedy, they knew that my love and respect for them were genuine, yet they also knew that as a Christian, I disagreed with their sexual behavior. In our friendship we could differ. The surviving one is still a friend. If I had merely "tolerated" them, we never could have gotten close enough to be friends.

The Bible teaches that God loves us exactly the way we are — but He loves us too much to want us to remain as we are. He wants us to change, to grow into the greatest possible fullness of character. Following His example, Christians take a stand for what we believe is right, especially regarding moral character and religious teaching. We love others as they are, but we believe we all could be more.

Therefore we speak of standards of behavior and lifestyle. Some have interpreted this as intolerance. But tolerance is not the point — it's too weak a word to spend time worrying about. Love and respect are much stronger ways of relating with each other, and the only way to break down the walls between us.

November 9, 2005; previously published in the Newport News Daily Press.

An Open Letter to Mental Health Professionals on "Tolerance"

Here's another way of making the point I was making in the previous essay. Tolerance is a weak, wimpy virtue. It's actually a harmful approach to treating people. Its effect is to stunt character growth. In some cases, it's even demeaning. This "open letter" is in response to something reported out of a psychology classroom at the University of Central Florida, where I went to grad school. I do not know Professor Negy, however.

Dear Mental Health Professional:

I write to you today as an inside-outsider related to your profession. I hold an M.S. in Industrial and Organizational Psychology. I make no pretensions to being qualified for mental health counseling, yet I am hardly unaware of the field.

I want to address you on disastrous mental health correlates that I think you would agree may be associated with today's understanding of "tolerance." I urge you to speak up as a profession and object to the promotion of tolerance as a virtue. It really is no virtue at all.

It stunts individuals' character growth and it hinders the development of meaningful interpersonal relationships. It stunts growth by falsely raising individuals' expectations that they will not experience conflict, and by falsely suggesting that they cannot face it if it comes.

An Illustration from a Psych Class
I illustrate with a 2012 incident in a psych class at my grad school alma mater, the University of Central Florida. Some students had spoken up in class in support of what they considered to be the

truth of their Christian beliefs. The professor, Charles Negy, responded with an email to the entire class, saying in part,

> Bigots ... are convinced their beliefs are correct. For the Christians in my class who argued the validity of Christianity last week, ... it seems to have not even occurred to you ... as I tried to point out in class tonight, how such bigotry is perceived and experienced by the Muslims, the Hindus, the Buddhists, the non-believers, and so on, in class, to have to sit and endure the tyranny of the masses (the dominant group, that is, which in this case, are Christians). [14]

Negy didn't use the word "tolerance" in his email, but his message is redolent of tolerance theory. The supposed virtue of tolerance is characterized by persons affecting agreement with others' views even when their own views differ — as if persons could hold contradictory views as being simultaneously true. It's characterized further by the insistence that if people do disagree, they must keep that to themselves.

This is consistent with what Negy called for on this occasion.

Four Points
I note four things here. None of it is particular to the target group's religion or to Christianity, the topic that had been under discussion. It applies to all relationships and all social groupings.

1. *Negy's use of shame to shape behavior.* It's an inherently other-diminishing approach, especially when applied by an authority figure. The call for tolerance often presents in a shame-based form.

2. *The protective attitude he takes with respect to Muslims, Hindus, etc.* He's treating them as though they will be harmed by

---

14   https://www.huffingtonpost.com/2012/08/16/charles-negy-reddit-letter-to-students_n_1789406.html

some students' disagreement, and as if they are unable to manage that harm on their own. But every person is destined to encounter disagreement, and should be prepared for it, not shielded from it.

3. *The interpersonal hiding his approach is designed to encourage.* Christians are shamed into hiding their core convictions. Other religious believers, and non-believers, too, are bound to get the message along with Christians. Either they will learn by example that they must hide their own central beliefs, or they follow the professor's example and shame their fellow students into silence. Neither approach is conducive to real relationships, between real people, being genuinely open with one another.

4. *The* acting-as-if *behaviors that the professor imposes upon the students.* Christians are told to act as if they don't hold their beliefs as true. Others are implicitly encouraged to do the same.

Peacekeeping vs. Peacemaking

There is a better approach to handling conflict. Undoubtedly you are aware of the distinction between the peacekeeper and the peacemaker. The peacekeeper is the enabler, the one who manages conflict by diverting, hiding, distracting, or otherwise avoiding. The peacemaker is the one who brings herself or himself fully into the conflict as a whole, entire person — or encourages others to do the same, if in a mediator's role — and seeks to lead the relationship toward integrity and peace at the same time.

Though the peacemaking approach does not always succeed in bring conflict to a halt, we know it's usually the best first approach to attempt. Peacekeeping is never our first advice — not unless there is immediate threat of lasting physical and/or emotional harm.

Now, Dr. Negy seems to imply that the non-Christian students in that classroom would be harmed to that degree by Christians communicating they think their beliefs are correct. *Surely, though, he*

221

cannot think Muslims, Hindus, Buddhists, and non-believers are that fragile. They aren't, except in the usual rare exceptional instances presumably occurring with equal frequency among all social groups. Still he has applied a peacekeeping, distance-making approach. This cannot be healthy as a first recourse.

Approaching, Loving, and Respecting vs. "Tolerating"

Peacemaking appreciates persons' differences rather than running from them. It encourages persons to respect others, even potentially to love them, in spite of differences. Loving respectfulness draws persons together as they are, not asking them to submerge or deny aspects of their core character, but rather to bring themselves into the open. If one's character needs correcting, it can be corrected in that kind of interaction.

If one's individual characteristics are worthy of appreciating (as is usually the case) they can be appreciated there — far more than if they're submerged under a veneer of pseudo-mutuality.

This, by the way, is what the word "tolerance" used to mean: It was never about acting as if we agree, it was about respecting and loving one another as persons whether we agree or not.

We don't hear much about love and respect in public conflict these days. These are the real virtues we should be encouraging, rather than the distance-producing counterfeit virtue of "tolerance."

I call upon the mental health professions to take up the call for interpersonal love and mutual respect, and to publicly identify contemporary "tolerance" as the false virtue it is, harmful to individuals and to relationships.

March 2, 2017

Practice What He Preached?

Some people think Jesus taught tolerance the way it's taught to-day. They've got a mixed-up view of him.

The other day I noticed a bumper sticker on it that I had never seen before. It had Jesus' face on it along with symbols from 15 different religions, and it read, "Practice what he preached." I was so intrigued, at the next red light I snapped this photo with my phone, but in case it's not quite readable I've added a close-up of the same.

The message is a restatement of the more familiar "Coexist," which this car was also displaying, except it adds another twist about its being what Jesus preached.

Jesus Didn't Actually Preach This

It is quite clear, though, that Jesus did not preach anything like "coexist" with respect to other religions. He warned his followers they would be hated for following him (Luke 6:22, John 15:18–25). When religious leaders had him killed, it sure wasn't because of some grand inclusiveness on his part. It was because he kept insisting they were wrong, both in doctrine and in deed.

And he did not say, "Have no enemies." He said, "Love your enemy." If that kind of love is what one means by "coexist," Jesus would undoubtedly agree. But he would insist that there is only one way, one truth, one life, and that he himself (and he only) is all of these (John 14:6).

In fact, Jesus was exclusivist to the point of paying the ultimate price. His death wasn't just the outcome of some failed relationship he had with religious leaders. It was what he came to do. In Gethsemane he prayed, "Is there any other way?" (Matthew 26:30–39). He knew the answer. He died for us precisely because there was no other way; all other religions are ways of deceit and death. There is life in Christ, and only in him.

It's Either Ignorance or Deception

This is the only Jesus of whom we have any historical record. Whence, then, comes a message like the one on this bumper sticker, so out of touch with evidence and reality? I can think of two possible sources: ignorance or deception.

It might be that whoever made up this message really thought this was what Jesus was all about. It's not hard: if you want to think of Jesus as history's grand teacher of tolerance, all you have to do is listen to popular misconceptions, and never bother to check the facts. But that's choosing ignorance — not just ordinary everyday ignorance, mind you, but ignorance with respect to the obvious. The historical record on Jesus is clear and transparent. To be this ignorant, a person would have to refuse to look.

Or it might be that the message is pure deception, springing from of the lying heart of some religious inclusivist who wants to co-opt Jesus to his or her cause. (I suppose it's also possible a person could do that out of self-deception.) If so, however, then why Jesus? Is the idea to poke at Christians, to provoke us to be more inclusivist "like Jesus"? But that's counting on us being ignorant. Any good liar ought to know better than that. It's a lousy deception in every way.

The message is a product either of willful ignorance or deception. Obviously so.

How *Do* We Practice What He Preached?

So obviously so, in fact, that I must ask myself, how can I *really* practice what Jesus preached at this point? What if I were to see this car at the grocery store this week, and have a chance to talk with the driver? What would I say? Should I pounce on her error? (I think it was a woman at the wheel.) No; I would want her to understand her error, but to experience that understanding through an encounter of love.

I would want to affirm her for putting Jesus at the center. I would ask, "What do you think Jesus actually preached?" If she was willing to answer, I would listen. I would ask how she came to that conclusion. (Readers of Greg Koukl's *Tactics* will recognize the questions.) I would ask her if she'd like to know more about what Jesus preached — in hopes she would come to know his truth and his life.

Compromise, No; Love, Yes

Final point, a question for myself: Am I that committed to genuine encounters of love with everyone on this blog? I'm a little worried about myself on that score. I have no love for deadly, deceptive error. Jesus didn't either. He opposed it forcefully enough to get himself killed over it. Still — what a great God we have! — he loved men, women, and children, including his enemies.

He never compromised. Still he loved.

Practice what he preached? I like that idea.

September 5, 2011

"I Identify as a Perfectly Tolerant Person"

This is the shortest piece in the book, and the most satirical. It's a snippet of a fictional dialogue set on some college campus that requires students and staff to be very tolerant of gender preferences, and to respect others' preferred pronouns. The "gender-transitioning" character speaks first.

"I've realized that I self-identify as a woman now. I'd like you to use female pronouns when you refer to me from now on."

"No, I'm going to keep referring to you as 'he' and 'him.'"

"But I'm saying that I'm a woman now. You need to use female pronouns with me."

"I'm saying no."

"That's terribly rude of you! I could report you to the administration for it."

"Really? How could it be rude? I identify as a perfectly courteous and tolerant person."

"But you aren't! You're refusing to use the pronouns I want you to use."

"My mental self-image says I am very tolerant, and very courteous."

"Your actions disprove it. You're rude."

"My mental self-image is the reality. I'm asking you from now on only to speak of me as a perfectly courteous and tolerant person."

"Oh, come on. I can't speak of you that way. Your mental self-image doesn't change the truth of what you are!"

"Oh, really? Is that true for sex and gender, too?"

March 18, 2017

Gay Rights and Rebellion
Against Human Nature

The gay rights movement isn't just a rebellion against standard morality. It isn't merely "tolerance" running wild. It's really an assault on human nature itself.

We may have missed the real truth about the LGBT rebellion against human nature. These are experimental thoughts that I'm only beginning to work on. You'll see the somewhat rambling effect of new thinking in process here. If you know of anyone who has written anything like this before me, I'd like to know about it.

Out of the Archives

But I was actually planning to write two other articles when this one popped out instead. The first was going to be one I ran across while randomly browsing files I had stowed away on disk here at home: Hadley Arkes's 1996 *First Things* article, "The End of Democracy? A Culture Corrupted." The whole thing is disturbingly prescient. I was tempted to quote entire paragraphs, but this is the one sentence that got me started.

> And one thing may be attributed to the gay activists quite accurately and fairly: they have the most profound interest, rooted in the logic of their doctrine, in discrediting the notion that marriage finds its defining ground in nature.[15]

Polygamy Arising

The second article (or trio of articles, actually) had to do with a Long Island case in which polygamy has achieved a new sort of quasi-legal status, through a judge granting three members of a

---

[15] https://www.firstthings.com/article/1996/11/005-the-end-of-democracy-a-culture-corrupted

throuple joint custody of a ten-year-old boy.[16] The NY Post even calls him "their" ten-year-old son.[17]

What does the son call his parents? We don't hear about the dad, but when the judge asked how he told his "moms" apart, he answered that "one was the 'mommy with the orange truck' and the other the 'mommy with the gray truck.'"

Christine Cauterucci, writing in *Slate,* called that answer "an adorable set of names more moms with trucks should adopt."[18] Really? More moms should consider it adorable to be identified as the parent with the red truck? Isn't there something more, you know, *personal* a child could know his or her mom by?

Part of our problem here is journalists getting stuck in "cute" when they should be thinking about what they're writing.

The Nature of Marriage

The bigger problem, though, is the one Arkes recognized 21 years ago: the attack against marriage having "its defining ground in nature." Until recently, marriage was thought to be a certain thing *by nature.* It had a reality, an essence of its own; it was what it was, not merely what the mood of the day (including this move toward legalized polygamy) said it was.

The Judeo-Christian line of thinking has considered marriage to be that way because God made it so. The attack on marriage has therefore always been partly an attack on religion.

---

[16]   http://whatswrongwiththe-world.net/2017/03/the_kids_are_not_okay.html
[17]   http://www.nypost.com/2017/03/10/historic-ruling-grants-custody-to-dad-and-mom-and-mom/
[18]   http://www.slate.com/blogs/xx_factor/2017/03/13/new_york_court_affirms_poly_parenthood_with_three_way_custody_ruling.html

But only partly, for marriage has always been known everywhere to be for man and woman, with or without the Judeo-Christian scriptures. Its natural meaning flowed directly from human nature. Marriage is what it is because humans are what we are.

Human Rebellion Against Nature

That's how we used to think of it; but humanity has rebelled against human nature. We've rebelled against nature itself: the nature of what it is to be human. But it's more complicated than that, for just what is it we're rebelling against?

There is human nature as we once thought of it: a real and stable essence that defined humanness. Just as marriage once used to be what marriage was, humans used to be what humans were.

Now, however, we refuse to be limited by what we are. Part of that refusal comes out in our unwillingness to let our physical sex limit either our genders or our relationships.

But human nature itself is complicated. How much is "human," and how much is "nature"?

Sex is biology, after all, and biology is nature; but mind is higher than nature and need not be limited by it. I'm sure some of us would choose to swim like fish if we could. We can't, obviously; some limits surpass all power of mind. But hey, we can declare our genders independently of our biology! We can devise our relationships without concern for nature's limitations, too.

Which brings me to the third source that came to mind this evening, leading to what I've got on my mind here. C.S. Lewis wrote the following in *The Abolition of Man* about man's drive to overcome Nature:

> From this point of view the conquest of Nature appears in a new light. We reduce things to mere Nature in order that we may 'conquer' them.... But as soon as we take the final step of reducing our own species to the level of Nature, the whole

process is stultified, for this time the being who stood to gain and the being who has been sacrificed are one and the same.

Human Nature as It Wasn't Meant to Be

Our drive to conquer nature impels us to rule over even that which is natural within us, wrote Lewis. He also saw the effect that would have: the conquerors would be at the same time the conquered.

For we are by nature (or so we are told) only natural. Let me say it again another way, so I won't be using "nature" in two different ways in the same sentence: We're convinced that we have no essence, no reality, except for what comes from, what remains, and what unavoidably and forever *is and shall be* the same sort of thing as the animals, the plants, and the soil we all spring from.

Which brings me finally to the point where I am beginning to wonder whether we conservatives have been getting the marriage and gender revolution all wrong — or at least, wrong insofar as we've thought it was a rebellion against human nature. I wonder if it might instead be the result of people *trying to live up to true human nature,* when they've been inculcated with a doctrine that there is no such thing.

Could LGBT Be Rebelling Against the Right Thing?

Make no mistake: we are *not* merely natural, and we all know it, in our inner and most human places. The merely-natural view is false. It deserves any rebellion that's raised up against it. In fact, given that we know better on the inside, it's impossible to imagine humans *not* rebelling against it.

Which makes me wonder: could it be the LGBT revolution is a rebellion against the right thing — though in the wrong way?

I think it's possible.

Yes, We Really Are Meant to Be More Than Our Biology

We were meant to be more than the merely-natural thing we've been told we are. We can't hide that reality from ourselves. The problem is, we don't know what that "more" could be. We know we were made to transcend, but we have no idea where we could possibly rise to. We're afraid we might really be stuck inside nature.

We sense that we were meant to be more than our biology. But our biology is all we are and all we have, or so we're told. Our one escape is to the least nature-like thing about us, our thoughts. So, we try to bootstrap ourselves right out of our biology by sheer mind-power. We flail, trying to punch our way out of a box that has no outside, as far as we know.

Maybe it's because sex is such a transcendent experience that it has become the sphere in which we have tried to ascend outside ourselves. It's still biology, though. That soaring feeling can be explained by neurochemical processes. As far as true humanness goes, it only lifts us high enough to think it's "adorable" when a ten-year-old tells his mommies apart by the colors of their trucks.

The Box Has to Have an Outside

That's about as far as any human experience can take us, as long as we refuse to see that the box has an outside after all. If nature is all humans are — if we can't see there's a reality outside the box — then we're stuck. Inside here we will continue to flail. And fail.

But if we can see that the box has an outside — that there's more to us than what's merely natural — then we can know our deepest human self-awareness is true. We can be who we are and what we are, both on the inside and the outside. We can be fully human, spirit, soul, and body, without needing to distort ourselves on any of those levels.

Getting on the Same Side of the (Human) Table

I'm not saying this is the full explanation for the LGBT revolution. There's a lot more nature-and-nurture going on than what I've focused on here. Sex itself is certainly part of it. Pride is, too, along with a host of social and spiritual factors I'll nod at in passing by way of tacit acknowledgement.

I'm also definitely not saying that the LGBT revolution is good just because it's a rebellion against the right thing. The 1917 Bolshevik rebellion in Russia was also at least partly against the right thing. The Czars were corrupt; but the Communism that followed it was, too, in completely new ways, and to unheard-of degrees.

Yet I think there's something here worth considering. Practically speaking, if it's true it could be a way to get on the same side of the table with LGBT people for a change:

"You want to rebel? What are you really rebelling against? Is it against being limited by your biology? Christians don't believe we're limited by what's merely natural, either. But we do think we're meant to be an integral whole, body, soul, and spirit. Wouldn't you like that for yourself, too?"

March 27, 2017

Rhetorical Strategy in the Marriage Debate

There are two fronts in the current debate over marriage and sexual morality. One has to do with the question, "Which side is right?" The other has to do with, "Who's more effective at convincing people that they're right?" In my view there's no question the traditional biblical view is much more right, but we've been way less effective in persuading people of it. Here's part of the reason why.

Activist Theodore Shoebat recently contacted thirteen gay or pro-gay bakers and asked them to bake a pro-traditional marriage cake with the words, "Gay Marriage Is Wrong" on it. He writes, "Each one denied us service, and even used deviant insults and obscenities against us. One baker even said that she would make me a cookie with a large phallus on it."[19]

It was a nice try at making a point. Surely it seems to reveal something, but even Christians have raised doubts as to the wisdom of the approach. A man and woman's wedding cake should be about their wedding. To expect it to do something else, like Shoebat's proposed cake, seems offensive even with respect to their own marriages, which confuses the experiment too much to allow for clear-cut conclusions. It leaves some wiggle room for alternate explanations, and in this case, "some" wiggle room is a lot.

---

[19]   http://freedomoutpost.com/2014/12/christian-man-asks-thir-teen-gay-bakeries-bake-pro-traditional-marriage-cake-denied-service/

Strategies

Still the experiment provides an excellent illustration of the rhetorical asymmetry between the pro-natural marriage position and the pro-gay "marriage" view. What I mean by *asymmetry* is that the communication and persuasion challenges faced by either side of this issue are really quite different. In this article I will first analyze that rhetorical asymmetry, and then offer advice as to how natural marriage proponents should take it into account. The lessons remain valid even after the Supreme Court's decision allowing gay marriage in 2015.

Here's the problem in a nutshell:

Every gay marriage wedding cake, no matter how it's decorated, says the man-woman-only view of marriage is wrong. But it takes special effort to make a man and woman's wedding cake communicate that gay marriage is wrong.

That's just symbolic of the problem, of course. Let me explain now what it means.

Rhetorical Strategy: People vs. an Abstraction

The marriage debate takes place on two levels, micro and macro. There is each pair of persons, each couple, wanting to marry; and there is the overall institution of marriage.

Same-sex "marriage" proponents are attacking an institution and defending couples' desires to marry. Natural marriage proponents are defending an institution and standing in the way of gay couples' desire to marry.

Natural-marriage proponents seek to disrupt two real people's desires, hopes, and felt needs. Same-sex marriage proponents seek to disrupt the historic institution of marriage.

So it's either defending couples or defending an institution. Rhetorically and persuasive, those who defend the couples, the actual living persons, have the natural advantage.

236

Natural-marriage proponents are cast as hating gays. That's real rhetorical trouble. Suppose, however, same-sex marriage advocates hate the man-woman-only view of marriage, though, and suppose their hatred for it is real. So what? Institutions aren't people. They're abstractions. How much trouble can a person get into for hating an abstraction?

Make no mistake: institutions matter. They matter to people. Marriage matters to children. It matters to communities and whole societies, *all of which are made up of people.* So it certainly isn't that the natural marriage position has no impact on people. It's that it's harder to take a picture of those people. It's harder to demonstrate how important marriage is to them — *even though it is.*

Rhetorical Strategy in the Central Issues

So then, from a rhetorical perspective, which of these plays better in the media?

The couple pointedly looking their debate opponent in the eye, and saying, "You don't want us to marry and experience the same kind of joys you experience in marriage. You must hate us to feel that way!"

Or,

The natural marriage proponent pointedly looking the gay or lesbian couple in the eye, and saying, "You're tearing down the central institution that holds society together!"

And what about this one, also from natural-marriage proponents?

"Gay marriage is morally wrong."

There's not much persuasive pull there, even if it's true. Which it is. The reason is because over the past few generations, right and wrong themselves have become seen as abstractions, dependent on institutions, authority structures, and "society" or "culture," whatever that might be.

So when man/woman-only marriage proponents stand up against same-sex marriage advocates, often we're seen as representing abstract institutions, while they're representing flesh-and-blood people.

What Works Trumps What's Right (Rhetorically, That Is)

Notice now how little of what I've said so far has anything to do with whether one side or the other is more nearly right. Gay "marriage" doesn't have to be right to win rhetorically. It has the strength of battlefield position and firepower.

Armies with superior strategic positions don't always have the superior moral position. Granted, some people hold to the theory that right and wrong depend on who wins. That would be an awkward position for gay-rights advocates to adopt: If right and wrong depended on who was holding the power, then when they started their campaign decades ago, they were wrong.

I won't dwell on that absurdity, though, because I don't accept the power premise on which it's based. When gay rights advocacy kicked in back in the late 60s and 70s, it was either right or wrong in itself, regardless of where it stood in relation to the culture's power structures.

And my point here again is that it didn't have to be right in order to win. That goes a long way toward explaining how it has been winning of late.

Real Strategy: To Be Both Effective and Right

We natural marriage proponents, then, are fighting this battle from an extremely difficult rhetorical position. We ask gay bakers to make cakes for us that express our position, just as gays have asked some of us to back cakes that express their position. Their request comes across as rhetorically natural, ours is clumsy and awkward. That's not Theodore Shoebat's fault. It's inherent in the structure of the debate. So what do we do?

First, we need to do our homework, and understand the reasons for our position. If you don't know why you stand for a natural marriage viewpoint, then I have trouble myself understanding why you would hold to it — even though I think you're right.

We do ourselves no favors by encouraging people to join our side thoughtlessly. This isn't just about rhetoric after all. I'm all for effectiveness, *but only with integrity.* If I had to choose, I'd rather be morally right than be the winner of this debate. Better yet, I'd like to be right and also effective.

Identify the Other Side's Rhetorical Weaknesses

Their clearest weakness to me is their dependence on dehumanizing rhetoric. When defending their own position, they can present a positive, sympathetic face. When they attack opposing views, they resort far too often to prejudice, stereotyping, and labeling.[20]

There are some strange contradictions in their position as well, and on these they are quite vulnerable. I'll name three examples:

- When they cast disagreement as hatred, for example, they label themselves as haters, for they disagree with us as much as we do with them.

- Their central talking point, "marriage equality," is one they themselves don't really believe in.[21]

- They call for major legal differentiations between same-sex friends who are having sex and those who are not, thus encouraging governmental oversight of sexual relationships — while also crying out, "Get the government out of my bedroom!"

---

[20]   https://www.thinkingchristian.net/posts/2010/11/to-treat-one-another-as-humans/
[21]   https://www.thinkingchristian.net/posts/2012/11/phil-and-alex-on-marriage-equality/

Be Wiser on Finding Points of Rhetorical Advantage

I applaud Theodore Shoebat's attempt to show gay bakers' discriminatory attitudes toward Christians, except I'm not sure he really did that. He asked bakers to make cakes introducing an attacking, negative message into an otherwise positive and joyful celebration, which bakers could easily have rejected just on the grounds that it was weird! (They didn't have to be as offensive as they were in their answers, though. There was more going on there than what I'm very charitably trying to offer them credit for.)

No, we should be asking gays to make cakes and cater events (conferences or seminars, perhaps) celebrating the positive value of what stand for: the institution of marriage for a man and a woman only. If they refuse, then that's clearly discriminating, without much room to wiggle out of the charge.

Put Real Faces on Our Position; Moral Truth

We need to feature adult children of same-sex couples, for example.[22] *Even though it's an uphill battle, we need to continue to explain and defend moral truth.*

Pray

Finally, and most importantly, we need to bear in mind that there is a spiritual asymmetry here as well. This whole article has been about rhetorical situations and strategy, but there are deep spiritual reasons to stand for natural marriage, and spiritual ways to do so: with love, with the truth, with prayer, never forgetting that Jesus Christ is at the center of all reality, including our lives and lives of those with whom we are debating.

February 20, 2014

---

[22]   http://www.thepublicdiscourse.com/2012/08/6065/

Ethics and Morality

Finally, to wrap up, three articles on ethics and freedom, not otherwise connected to one another.

The "Whatever" Problem With "Jesus Never Excluded Anyone"

Many Christian (or formerly Christian?) churches have jumped on the pro-LGBT bandwagon. They see it as an important way to build loving connections to our culture. "Jesus never excluded anyone," after all. That's true in one way, but very dangerously wrong in another.

It came up again this weekend: a church leader saying, "We must not side with those in the church who would exclude a certain group of people. Jesus never excluded anyone."

Of course, we all knew what issues he was talking about.

Yet there's a bigger problem with this statement of his than either the group or the issue. So I'm not going to name it either.

I know you'll know what I'm referring to. What I write here could apply equally as well to other issues, though, in other times and places. *This post isn't about that specific issue; it's about Christians' dangerous tendency to bend their view of Scripture to accommodate current cultural demands, whatever those demands may be.*

I have three points. First, the idea that Jesus never excluded any-one is both careless and almost entirely false. Second, this way of thinking usurps God's place, putting humans in charge of our re-lationships with him. Third, it tends to set aside the most central fact of Christianity — redemption through the cross — as if it were hardly relevant.

243

1. "Jesus Never Excluded Anyone" Is a Careless and Generally False Statement

The Church *should* indeed welcome everyone. There's no denying that.

The Church has never fully practiced that welcome. There's no denying that, either.

But hold on a moment: what do we mean by "welcome"? Can we use a little care in defining our terms, please?

If we mean the Church should invite everyone into a loving, truth-filled, warmly-offered opportunity to seek God together with us, then yes, we should welcome everyone.

Often, however, this statement means everyone may be welcomed into full communion and fellowship as members of the people of God, including positions of church leadership. For those who take the Bible seriously — who look to the evidence to determine whether Jesus excluded anyone or not — this is obviously false.

Jesus pointedly excluded the scribes and Pharisees (see all of Matthew 23). He obviously excluded certain ideas and beliefs, including the belief that what follows below is optional.

The rest of Scripture supports what I'm saying, for example 1 Cor. 6:9–10. Incidentally, this leader who tried to say Jesus never excluded anyone made that point in the course of a talk based on the first chapter of that same book of the Bible. Surely, he knows that God's word includes more than the red letters!

Also in 1 Corinthians, Paul very pointedly excluded a man who claimed to be a brother in Christ but was practicing immorality (1 Cor. 5:1–5). The reason Paul did that, the passage says, is so "his spirit may be saved in the day of the Lord." Exclusion from fellowship is a signal, a warning sent to unrepentant sinners, telling them it's wrong to think they're at one with the people of Christ while they persist in open disobedience to God.

Conversely, then, to allow people into full fellowship (including leadership) while they persist in open disobedience is to send them a false signal that everything's okay. It's like saying, *"Hey, whatever, we don't care. It doesn't matter."* It paves the way to their spirit's destruction. *For that reason, it's not the least bit loving. It's deadly*

2. It Usurps God's Place as God in Our Relationships with Him

The error that "Jesus never excluded anyone" may come from confused thinking the truth that he *invited* everyone. He made it very clear that all are welcome in his kingdom. It's fine and good to affirm that. The *error* associated with it comes from forgetting that he extends his invitation *on his terms*.[23] And it comes as well from forgetting that we are welcome specifically on his terms. See for example Matt. 8:18–22 and Mark 10:17–22.

This is no small error. God does have the right, doesn't he, to determine how we relate to him? He is Creator, he is King, and he is holy. Nothing could be clearer in Scripture. It's equally plain to see that he has standards for us, and that one's relationship with him depends on how one responds to those standards.

To say "everyone is welcome" without conditions is to ignore God's own word on the matter.

3. It Makes the Cross of Christ Irrelevant

The leader I'm referring to could have said: "We shouldn't exclude this group because their uniquely characteristic actions are fine. They aren't wrong." That would be one kind of error, in my considered opinion. He didn't say that, though. He made a different kind of mistake instead. Besides the two problems I've already mentioned, this message tends to invalidate the purpose of the cross. That's a huge error in my book; it strikes at the very

---

23   See https://stream.org/god-loves-you-no-exceptions-his-terms/

core of our faith. But I need to explain how I think this makes the cross irrelevant.

A. If it's clear (and it is) that our relationship with God depends on how we respond to godly standards, then what response does he require? It isn't perfection, that's for sure. No one but Jesus even comes within sight of that mark. What he wants us to do instead is acknowledge our imperfections — our sin, that is — and trust in Christ to forgive us through his redemption on the cross.

B. What he doesn't want us to do is to tell people, "Hey, it doesn't matter what you do, since Jesus includes everyone." The cross of Christ *proves* that it matters what we do: Christ *died* to redeem us and forgive us of what we've done wrong.

C. The test this leader gave for including this group had nothing to do with rightness or wrongness. It was just this: "Jesus doesn't exclude anyone." Period.

D. Now, if we should include all persons just for that reason, then just as our doing so doesn't depend on their being wrong, it also doesn't depend on their being right. Right and wrong have nothing to do with it. This approach simply *sets aside* rightness or wrongness.

E. But to set aside rightness or wrongness on any contentious issue, where that's at least an open question, is to say, "Hey, whatever; rightness or wrongness don't matter on this point, so what you do doesn't matter, since Jesus includes everyone."

F. And that's wrong; it makes the cross irrelevant (see B).

Now what I said above is that this *tends* to make the cross irrelevant. I left some room in there for the possibility that this leader might say, "Hold on a minute! I'm not ignoring the cross! I just didn't have time to tell you the whole story. I've done the work, and I'm convinced these actions are perfectly in tune with God's will." In that case he could still be honoring the cross; he'd be making a different mistake instead. But he didn't state it that way.

These are really dangerous errors for church leaders to make, regardless of the specific issue of the day.

June 12, 2017

Can You Become a Better Person?

This essay's purpose is to show that moral relativism — the idea that morals depend on the person's beliefs, or the culture of the day — leads to some pretty ridiculous conclusions. Therefore, it really can't be true at all.

If what you want is really to become a better person, though, the opening sections of this book are more what you're looking for.

Is it possible to become a better person: more moral, more ethical? Undoubtedly yes, if we know what *"a better person"* means. It can be shown, however, that under moral relativism that concept doesn't actually have a usable definition. So, is it possible to become a better relativist? I can't see how!

That's not to say that moral relativists cannot become better persons. But they can't do it under their own terms of morality. They can only become better in ways that borrow from other views of morality, including Christian theism.

Relativists' intuition or knowledge of personal growth is rationally at odds with their philosophy. It is so much at odds that if their philosophy were correct, then no one's belief that they were growing ethically could ever be true.

To show this, I first need to set some definitions in order.

Moral Relativism and Moral Realism
Moral relativism is, broadly speaking, the belief that there is no transcendent, fixed anchor point for right and wrong. Right and wrong are up to individuals, societies, or cultures to decide for themselves. As they change, right and wrong can change with them. Therefore, what is actually, truly, right in one place or for one person can be actually, truly wrong for another culture.

Let's set this against the familiar concept that tastes and customs are locally determined. Tibetans eat everything with their fingers (no forks, spoons, or chopsticks). In Japan, a good belch after a meal sends a welcome message that you really enjoyed the food. These things which are right in those places are socially unacceptable in places where the cultural heritage is European. But that's very familiar; nothing controversial there.

Moral relativism is similar. It says that just as belching or eating with one's fingers may be right or wrong depending on context, so *any* other human choice may be right or wrong, depending on context. If a tribal culture believes sacrificing children to the "gods" is right, then in their tribe it is. If you and I believe it's wrong here, then it's wrong here. It's all a matter of context.

The Christian theist position stands in stark contrast to that. Christian ethics involve *moral realism:* the belief that moral principles exist independently of human beliefs or opinions; there are at least some things that are actually right or wrong, and would be right or wrong even if every human had the wrong opinion. This if every person and every culture thought that sacrificing children to the "gods" was right, it would still be wrong anyway. For Christians, real morality is grounded in the character of God.

A Sense of Direction

When my children were very young, they only thought of their own needs, and they were quite demanding about them. Now (ages 12 and 16, as of this [2007] writing) they put others' concerns first quite regularly. They have a way to go yet, to be sure, but they're maturing.

Now, *growing* and *maturing* are both directional terms. Physical growth is in the direction of larger, heavier, etc. Mental growth is in the direction of having more knowledge, more capacity to process ideas, etc. Maturing is not just about getting older, but about moving in a direction considered to be more wise, knowledgeable, and so on.

249

So when we speak of moral growth or maturation, we automatically think directionally. We think of a person moving toward being guided by better principles, holding to a better standard, thinking and living more in conformity to some higher ethic.

The Personal View

Now consider yourself: Can you become a better person, morally? The relativist position says that what is right for you is what you have decided is right for you. You have the privilege to determine right and wrong for yourself, and presumably you have done so: You've defined right and wrong for yourself.

But it's hard on that basis to see how you can be more right than you already are, if where you are now is right. There's no direction for you to move in; no "bigger" or "larger" (using physical analogies); there is no "ethically wiser" for you to move toward. For in order for "ethically wiser" to exist, there must be something existing that is actually more or less wise.

And of course, *wise* is not equivalent to *learned*. It's at least arguable that certain anti-human professors like Peter Singer or Ward Churchill, although quite learned, are not examples of ethical wisdom; or at least if they are, then *wisdom* becomes another directionless word, so we cannot use it to provide our needed sense of direction for moral growth.

So, what could moral growth possibly mean under relativism? Let's consider some options.

Maybe it means resolving personal inconsistencies. Suppose I believed it was right to sacrifice children to the "gods" for the sake of next year's harvest, and yet I also believed every child's life was of more value or worth than any crop could be. Then I'd have an inconsistency to resolve. One of those beliefs ought to give way to the other, if not for moral reasons then at least for logical ones.

So then, which of those two beliefs — the child is more important than the crop, or vice-versa — should we set aside for the sake of logical consistency? If we take them individually and relativistically, it's hard to see which one, by itself, is more moral than the other. Which one comes closer to the true moral standard? Who knows, when the individual sets the standard? Whatever the person decides, that decision is right! It would have to come down to some subjective opinion, maybe the choice that the person considers more ethically compelling.

(One might object that these are larger than individual issues; they extend to whole cultures. But my illustration here could be enlarged to whole cultures just as easily as that.)

Morally Compelling
But what is this "morally compelling" thing about? It could be a gut feeling; it could be the local customs; it could even be whatever gives the person a sense of permission to do what she wanted to do anyway. (I suspect there's a lot of that going on in moral relativism.)

But in the case of our child sacrifice example, either choice could be morally compelling. If one kills the child for the sake of the crops, that could certainly be as moral (on relativism) as deciding to save the child and risk the crops. So, if someone who decided midlife that he ought to save the child has grown morally, you couldn't call that a morally higher position, because there's no directionality there. There's no "higher" there to grow toward.

And what if he comes to understand there's no relationship after all between such acts of sacrifice and the success of his crops? He might change his practice, but that's not moral growth. It's more of an economic transition; the recognition that there's no benefit related to the cost.

The Challenge to Relativists

But that's too theoretical. Let's go to an actual current controversy of which [in 2007] embryonic stem cell research (ESCR) is as good as any. One side of the debate says harvesting human embryos is a kind of child sacrifice: killing helpless innocents for the sake of older, more responsible persons. The other side says it's wrong to embryos in that way.

Who's right? Who knows? Relativism has no moral reference point from which to decide.

I disapprove of ESCR, but suppose we had a long debate and you convinced me that ESCR was good after all. That would be moral *change* for me, but not moral *improvement.* How could we say that I was, since we don't know what "morally better" means?

Or let's suppose again that you convinced me that homosexual practice was a morally neutral matter, so that practicing homosexual relationships could be just as moral as heterosexual marriage relationships. Again, for me that would be a (very large!) change in my moral opinion, but in what way have I become morally better for having changed? What does "better" mean in that context?

My challenge to relativists is for them to define *"morally better"* in a way that actually makes moral growth a coherent principle within their system of thought. I don't believe they can do it.

It's up to relativists, to show how moral change could ever mean morally growth; but I can't see how the can do that from within a coherent moral relativist framework.

I am quite sure relativists grow morally over your years of life, but I believe it takes moral realism for that actually to make sense.

*Let's set aside for now whether our presumed duty to be logically consistent is a *moral* duty. That's at least a possibility, and if true, then it muddies these waters considerably. It certainly

252

wouldn't help the relativist position! My point here does not require us to resolve that, though.

December 17, 2007

Three Reasons Freedom of Religion Matters

Finally, to close the book, an essay on a topic of crucial importance to all Christians everywhere.

Freedom of religion matters. It is unique from other freedoms. Its choice for inclusion in the Bill of Rights wasn't made for merely *ad hoc* reasons. Specifically, freedom of religion is not freedom-of-something-or-other.

I needed to say that when I saw a comment today in response to the statement that at least two people in the UK had lost their jobs for opposing gay marriage,

> Okay, but that's not the issue. If they lost their jobs for discriminating against people who are black, or disabled, or something, who would be crying about "freedom: — then? (I wish I could refuse to do my job and not get sacked, on the basis of my freedom-of-something-or-other!)

Of course, I agree that freedom of religion doesn't mean always being able to fall back on one's faith as a reason not to do one's job. Sorting that out can be complicated, but that's not my purpose here. What I want to say instead as that freedom of religion differs from other freedoms (freedom of something-or-other in at least three fundamental aspects.

1. Dethroning the state
Freedom of religion signifies the state's recognition that it's not the highest power. Even Benjamin Franklin, noted non-believer, assured the Continental Congress that "God rules in the affairs of men."

This recognition is basic to all other human liberties. The state is the highest earthly power, and as such, it is subject to all the temptations of power. Governments expand to fill the space available. There are only two effective checks upon their growth, and ultimately their intrusion upon all subjects and citizens. The first such check is another competing human power: another state or the state's own citizenry. The second is the sober awareness that they are not the highest power after all; that they answer to another, higher Power.

Totalitarianism runs shoulder-to-shoulder with institutionalized unbelief. The twentieth century was overrun with examples. Squashing religion serves the authoritarian state's interest: it's called "eliminating competition for the throne." The best defense against this illiberal outcome is freedom of religion.

2. Freedom of conscience
The state has a certain stake in individuals' consciences. Conscience is part of the point of legislation, which should be both a reflection and a guide for public conscience. So then, for example, to the extent that the state approves gay "marriage," it is telling its people that men and women of good conscience will or should approve it as well.

To this, however, there must be a limit. It's one thing for the state to encourage good conscience with respect to murder, theft, kidnapping, and so on. It's another thing for the state to enforce (read: to "force") actions in conflict with long-established matters of conscience like marriage and morality.

3. Religion as conscience to the state
The first two points intersect in religion's vital role of speaking truth to power.

Religion should not hold temporal power; that sort of relationship always goes to seed. Religion does its best public policy work in tension with the state, and likewise, the state does its best work in tension with religion. The state needs contrary voices, to keep it in good conscience. Of all possible such voices, religion has the greatest potential to stand in an independent position, not beholden to government, and not dependent on government for its ethics, principles, and values.

Who dares stand up against the potentially massive power of the state, after all? It's the one who recognizes the greater power of God

The state will not always appreciate religion's contrary voice. Conscience can be quite a bother to individuals; why not also to the government? So the state will often be tempted to still that voice by limiting religious expression, mandating that it remain private, dismissing it as mere "belief," and otherwise sweeping it aside. To allow the state to succeed in that, however, would be to promote the state's governing with a seared conscience. It would be disastrous to more freedoms than just religion.

June 1, 2013

About the Author

Tom Gilson is a Senior Editor and Ministry Coordinator with *The Stream* (https://stream.org). His 200-plus published articles have also appeared at *BreakPoint* Online, in *Salvo, Touchstone,* and *Discipleship Journal* magazines, and in the *Washington Post.* Previous books include *True Reason: Confronting the Irrationality of the New Atheism* (Kregel, 2013), for which he was the lead editor, *Critical Conversations: A Christian Parents' Guide to Discussing Homosexuality With Teens* (Kregel, 2015); as well as the self-published *Peter Boghossian Atheist Tactician: A Preliminary Response to A Manual for Creating Atheists* (2013) and *How Would Jesus Blog? Answering Online Adversaries Jesus' Way* (2017).

Tom is a regular speaker at the annual Defend Conference, New Orleans Baptist Theological Seminary, and has spoken often at other national conferences including Truth for a New Generation and the National Conference on Christian Apologetics.

Tom's started out as a musician, then moved quickly into missionary training work with Campus Crusade for Christ (now Cru), which was probably at that time (and still may be) the world's largest non-denominational missions organization. For much of the 1990s he served as a senior leader on Cru's joint HR director team, where he became known as an expert in personnel problem resolution, working and resolving issues reaching as high as the U.S. Capitol in Washington, D.C.

Later he was named Director of Strategic Operations on a team reporting to Cru's board of directors, doing internal consulting in strategy and organizational effectiveness, and providing advice and support to Cru's internal auditors. Following that he served two years as a strategy specialist on loan with Chuck Colson's BreakPoint ministry, then transitioned to a couple of years working first as national field director, then vice president in the newly-developing apologetics campus ministry Ratio Christi.

Now, though, his heart is with the local church. He knows that issues in our own communities can be every bit as significant as in the Hart Senate Office Building.

As time allows, he offers his expertise to churches and other ministries for consulting on personnel issues and team dynamics. He practices a dual specialty: walking with ministries through problems that seem unsolvable, and (better by far) working with them to avoid and prevent "unsolvable" situations. He holds an M.S. in Industrial and Organizational Psychology (University of Central Florida, 1998).

And of course, he is a writer who loves to speak the greatness, goodness, and truth of God in Jesus Christ. But by now you know about that.

Tom grew up in Michigan, studied trombone at Michigan State University, married his beloved Sara in 1987, and is seeing the joy of his two adult children not only walking in Christ, but also both becoming happily married within a short 8-month space of time in 2017 and 2018. He lives near Cincinnati, Ohio.

Contact Tom for speaking or consulting at tomgilson.org.